The World's Wildest Waters

Written by
Catherine Barr

Illustrated by
Riley Samels

Contents

Map 4–5
Introduction 6–7

Coral reefs
The Cook Islands 8–11
The Cook Islands is a country made up of 15 islands in the South Pacific. Explore the shallow waters and discover more about the colorful reefs.

Waterfalls
Angel Falls 12–15
Venezuela is home to Angel Falls, the world's highest uninterrupted waterfall at almost 3,281 ft (1,000 m) tall. Get up close and feel the spray of the cool water.

The Pacific Ocean
The White Shark Café 16–19
Dive into the largest and deepest ocean on Earth, and discover a secret location that few people know about…

Wetlands
The Okavango Delta 20–23
The Okavango Delta in Botswana is the world's largest inland delta. Here you'll meet some of Earth's most endangered large mammals.

Kelp forests
Sussex 24–27
Kelp forests can be found along England's southeast coast. Take a swim through this incredible rewilding project.

Tributaries
Chambal River 28–31
The Chambal River starts in the hills near Mandav, India, and flows to join the Yamuna River in Jalaun. Look out for snapping gharials as you wind along.

The Weddell Sea
The Endurance shipwreck 32–35
More than 9,869 ft (3,000 m) under the surface of the Weddell Sea lies the shipwreck of *Endurance*. Navigate around its ghostly decks and cabins.

Micro-aquatic habitats
The Amazon rainforest 36–39
The Amazon rainforest spans 2.1 million sq miles (5.5 million sq km). Crouch down and get up close to the tiny creatures that call this lush habitat home.

Oceanic islands
Ascension Island 40–43
Ascension Island is a remote volcanic island in the Atlantic Ocean between Brazil and Southern Africa. Trek its sandy beaches and forested slopes.

Lakes
Lake Titicaca 44–47
In the Andes mountains lies Lake Titicaca—the world's highest navigable lake. You might find more than you expected in its hidden depths…

Archipelagos
The Galápagos Islands 48–51
The Galápagos Islands are a collection of 19 islands surrounded by a marine reserve. Keep your eyes open for scaly iguanas and scuttling crabs in the shallows.

Lagoons
Namibian Islands' Marine Protected Area 52–55
In sub-Saharan Africa lies Namibia, the region's driest country. Float in the calm lagoon as flamingos honk and seabirds glide gracefully overhead.

Southern Ocean
Antarctic ice shelves 56–59
Also known as the Antarctic Ocean, the Southern Ocean is the most southerly of the world's oceans. Grab your wetsuit and dive into its cold depths.

Caves
The Cave of the Hanging Snakes 60–63
Deep in the Yucatán jungles in southern Mexico lies a cave that's like no other. Turn on your headlamp and step carefully into the mysterious darkness.

Gulfs
Sea of Cortez 64–67
The Sea of Cortez—"Mar de Cortés" in Spanish—separates the Baja California Peninsula and mainland Mexico. Say *hola* to these warm waters.

Bays
Jervis Bay 68–71
The whitest sand in the world can be found on the shores of Jervis Bay in New South Wales, Australia. Watch on as the waves glow and sparkle with life.

Mangroves
The Maldives 72–75
Twenty-six atolls make up the Maldives, one of the smallest countries in Asia. Paddle in the warm shallows of a tangled mangrove forest where sea creatures hide.

Endorheic basins
The Caspian Sea 76–79
Despite its name, the Caspian Sea isn't actually a sea but rather the largest salt lake in the world. Float past whiskery sturgeons and swans visiting for the season.

Arctic Ocean
Alaska 80–83
The Arctic Ocean is one of Earth's coldest oceans and also its least salty. Break through the ice shelves and discover life below the surface.

Rivers
Yellowstone River 84–87
The Yellowstone River is the only major undammed river in the contiguous United States. Spot animals great and small as you crash and course along it.

Glossary 88
Animal index 89–93

will you dive into today?

Foreword

In this book, you will find out about some amazing ocean creatures and other animals that dwell in freshwaters and seas around the world and hopefully be inspired to help protect them.

You will discover the tallest waterfall in the world, which is a magnet for crocodiles, anacondas, howler monkeys, and poisonous frogs. There's a shipwreck at the bottom of the sea that is home to starfish, humpback whales, and colossal squid. And who knew there was a secret café in the Pacific Ocean where the world's biggest sharks meet up for a bite to eat?

The amazing places these animals can be found in are a vital part of the cycle of life on Earth. They give us the water we drink and the oxygen we breathe. They also absorb carbon, which helps in the fight against climate change. Many of the wild waters featured here are under threat and need our protection.

© Matt Jarvis / Blue Marine Foundation

In this book, you will find out more about the people who are working to preserve these wild places for future generations. Even though coral reefs and African lagoons may be far from where you live, you will discover lots of ways to help protect them yourself. Tell your friends and family too—we can all make a difference.

Thank you to everyone who has helped create this book. It's now more important than ever that we protect the oceans. I hope you enjoy exploring the world's wildest waters in the pages to come.

Eugenie

HRH Princess Eugenie
Ambassador, Blue Marine Foundation

Who are Blue Marine Foundation?

BLUE MARINE FOUNDATION

Blue Marine Foundation is a UK-based marine conservation charity dedicated to protecting and restoring life in the ocean. Since being founded in 2010, they have made it their mission to see 30 percent of the world's ocean under effective protection and the other 70 percent responsibly managed by 2030. But how do they do this? Blue Marine creates marine reserves, restores important habitats, sets up models for sustainable fishing, and connects people with the sea.

Many of us know that the Earth's precious marine ecosystems are under pressure from threats including climate change, acidification, pollution, ocean noise, and invasive species. But Blue Marine believes the greatest threat of all is overfishing. The ocean's complex web of marine life enables it to absorb around a third of the world's carbon dioxide, so it is the Earth's largest carbon sink. The ocean also produces as much as half of our oxygen, so it is crucial that we all act now to protect much, much more of it.

A healthy ocean is particularly important for the billions of people who depend on seafood for protein and are most exposed to the negative impacts of climate change. Blue Marine works with international NGOs (Non-Governmental Organizations) on policy and with local NGOs and communities in our project locations. Their work spans 40 projects in 14 countries, and to date, Blue Marine has contributed to the protection of more than 1,544,409 sq miles (4,000,000 sq km) of the ocean—that's larger than England, France, and India combined!

Working alongside their projects, Blue Marine has eight specialist units, which they think of like the arms of an octopus. Through these units, Blue Marine's team identify the best way to help the ocean—be it media and education to raise awareness, policy and legal action to bring change, investigations and science to discover the truth, or innovative economics and climate studies to bring new ideas into marine conservation.

Throughout this book, you'll be traveling to some of Blue Marine's project locations to meet the wonderful creatures beneath the waves: from short-snouted seahorses and green turtles to elegant flamingos and grumpy groupers. You'll also get to explore the secret marine habitats these animals live in, from the UK's tangled kelp forests and the remote Ascension Island to the bustling mangroves of the Maldives and the landlocked Caspian Sea.

From Blue Marine and all its conservation partners around the world, thank you for picking up this copy of *The World's Wildest Waters* and taking the time to read about our work!

Blue Marine partners featured in this book are:
- Sussex Wildlife Trust
- Ascension Island Government
- Namibia Nature Foundation
- Maldives Resilient Reefs
- IDEA, Azerbaijan

The Cook Islands

In the middle of the Pacific Ocean, there's a place where the bright blue sky meets golden sand and turquoise sea. Beneath the surface are gardens of coral, shoals of colorful fish, sea turtles, sharks, and whales who all call this paradise home. There are predators and prey, and everything living in these sunlit waters is looking for a meal. A moray eel pokes its huge head out of a reef crevice to eye up passing fish. A tiger shark swerves suddenly to chase a sea turtle. The shark's huge shadow scatters the coral-nibbling parrotfish, and an octopus slithers back under a shell. As night falls, even the coral—which seem so still—stretch their tiny tentacles into the gentle current in search of food.

Habitat

The Cook Islands are 15 islands in the middle of the Pacific Ocean, far from land. One is the tip of an underwater volcano blanketed in lush forest. Some islands are simply sand, while others are warm, shallow lagoons fringed by coral reefs.

Fish nursery
Coral reefs provide a place for fish to live and grow

The reefs here are made from huge colonies of coral that grow into colorful, rocky underwater gardens. The sunlit waters and dark crevices are home to many endangered ocean animals as well as those stopping over on epic global migrations.

Hawksbill sea turtle
Hawksbills have sharp beaks to poke into coral reefs, looking for sponges to eat. These endangered turtles also crawl up the Cook Islands' sandy beaches to lay their eggs.

Albacore tuna
In the space of three months, a female albacore tuna can lay up to 3,000,000 eggs!

Coral reef

Coral are marine animals that build hard skeletons on their exterior to protect their soft bodies. They become fixed in one place and then slowly grow to create coral reefs. Coral live in all of the Earth's oceans, but they only build reefs in shallow, tropical waters.

Whale shark
This majestic spotted shark swims slowly, cruising through the warm, tropical waters of the South Pacific. But don't worry—this shark is gentle and playful and does not pose any threat to human divers.

Did you find them all?

Lionfish
This poisonous, spiky fish is a top predator in the coral reef. It is a deadly tropical hunter and an invasive species that destroys populations of other creatures living on the reef.

Black-lip pearl oyster

Oysters produce a liquid called nacre to protect themselves against irritants that get into their shells. Layers of nacre then form pearls.

Coconut crab

Coconut crabs do love coconuts! They use their claws to crack open the hard shells of coconuts so that they can eat the flesh inside.

Deep-sea mining destroys precious seabed habitats. Thankfully, special laws in the Cook Islands protect its waters from this activity. Laws here also prevent large-scale fishing, which saves sea turtles, sharks, and whales from being caught by mistake.

Honeycomb moray eel

Moray eels spend most of their time in the reef's deep, rocky holes. When they spot their prey, these giants slither out of the dark to hunt.

Staghorn coral

This endangered coral creates underwater gardens in orange, purple, and pink. Its branches are like the antlers of a deer and form sheltered places for fish to hide.

The people helping

Marine conservationist Jacqueline Evans has lived on the Cook Islands for many years, and she has been awarded a prize for her campaign to protect the waters around the islands. She works with local communities and fishers and has helped bring in new laws that will conserve and sustainably manage the islands now and in the future.

How you can help

Scientists have shown that the chemicals in many sunscreens can damage coral when they wash off our bodies into the sea. So next time you're taking a dip at the beach, ask your adult to use reef-safe sunscreen. The coral will thank you!

Great frigatebird

This huge black bird with a bright red pouch soars above the warm reef waters. Sometimes it surprises fishers by landing on the deck of their boats to steal a fishy snack.

Parrotfish

These shimmering fish help build beaches. Parrotfish nibble on coral, which is then ground up in their stomachs and comes out in their poop!

Angel Falls

Through the spray of the world's tallest waterfall, a harpy eagle soars on his enormous wings. This huge bird glides through the swirling, humid air and arcs across the foot of Angel Falls before landing on the branch of a tree. The dazzling sun glints off the sheer rock face of this extraordinary waterfall as the water of the great Churn River plunges downward and disappears into the pool below. Far above, under the cover of cloud, carnivorous plants lure insects into watery traps; and in rainforests that cloak the valley, poisonous frogs hop, snakes slither, and jaguars prowl.

Habitat

Angel Falls in Venezuela is part of the huge Orinoco River basin. Here, the Carrao River thunders over the cliffs of one of hundreds of flat-topped mountains in this remote, mostly unexplored land.

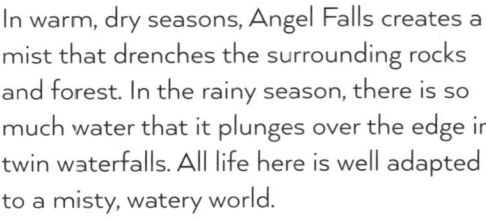

In warm, dry seasons, Angel Falls creates a mist that drenches the surrounding rocks and forest. In the rainy season, there is so much water that it plunges over the edge in twin waterfalls. All life here is well adapted to a misty, watery world.

Orinoco crocodile

The Orinoco crocodile is sociable but aggressive, so the strongest crocodiles are in charge. The females look after their young for up to three years to protect them from hungry males.

Rocky ledge This is also called an outcropping

Sundew plant
The sundew plant is a carnivorous plant, which means that it eats insects. When an insect lands, the sundew curls its sticky red leaf around its prey and digests it.

Plunge pool The crashing water can cause whirlpools

Waterfall

A waterfall is a body of water that plunges steeply over a rocky ledge and lands in a plunge pool below. There are lots of different types of waterfalls, including chutes (which have narrow streams of water), block waterfalls (which have wide streams of water), and multistep waterfalls (connected waterfalls that each have their own plunge pool).

May flower
The strong-scented May flower is an orchid and the national flower of Venezuela. More than 500 different types of orchids grow in the cloudy forests around Angel Falls.

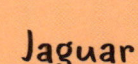

Giant anaconda
This scaly giant is the heaviest snake in the world. In water, it is sleek and fast, but it moves much more slowly on land.

Did you find them all?

Jaguar
Jaguars are South America's biggest predators, but they are difficult to find. In their thick jungle habitat, their rippling spotted coats keep them perfectly camouflaged.

Angel Falls lies in the Canaima National Park. The park is home to the Indigenous Pemón people who call it Kerepakupai Meru, which means "leap from the deepest place." Tourists must fly in or come on a long river journey to see this spectacular sight. But the rivers flowing through this dramatic landscape are threatened with pollution, and many endangered animals are illegally poached.

Harpy eagle
One of the world's largest eagles, the harpy can lift prey half its own body weight. It uses huge talons to snatch monkeys, snakes, and even a sleepy sloth.

Yellow-banded poison dart frog
Female yellow-banded poison dart frogs lay eggs out of the water, and then the male carries the tadpoles to puddles to grow.

Red howler monkey
Red howler monkeys are particularly chatty early in the morning. Their "dawn chorus" of howls and roars echoes for up to 3 miles (5 km)!

The people helping
The Pemón people are an Indigenous community who live in the Canaima National Park, where Angel Falls can be found. They act as tour guides, sharing stories about the waterfall and their relationship with it.

How you can help
Do your part to save water! It can be tempting to make your shower feel like a big, powerful waterfall, but try to keep it as short as possible. And remember to turn off the tap while you brush your teeth.

Reddish hermit hummingbird
Reddish hermit hummingbirds are one of the smallest birds in the world. The females weave their tiny nests under a drooping leaf at the forest's edge.

Roraima rocket frog
These tiny frogs are only about the size of a human's little finger, and they hide a little yellow stomach on their underside. Roraima rocket frogs are endemic to the high, flat-topped cliffs of Angel Falls.

The White Shark Café

Far from land, in a remote part of the Pacific Ocean, there is a place nicknamed the White Shark Café. In winter, the biggest sharks on Earth head to this mysterious marine hot spot. They set off from the Californian coast, full from feasting on elephant seals and sea lions, to gather in the open ocean. When the great white sharks arrive, the males begin their curious diving ritual. They plunge into the dark, icy waters over and over again, hunting for the squid that pulse through the ocean beyond the light.

Can you find them all?

Bioluminescent lanternfish

Medusa jellyfish

Ocean sunfish

Habitat

At first, scientists thought the White Shark Café was an ocean desert with little food for big predators. But far below the surface, the ocean was found to be teeming with squid, fish, crustaceans, and jellyfish that sharks like to eat.

Size
The Pacific Ocean is larger than the landmass of all the continents combined

The open ocean is a temporary home for migrating marine life on long journeys around the world. Super-speedy blue marlins leap through the swell, sea turtles pop up to breathe, and the deep shadows of great whales can be spotted from space.

Great white shark
The great white shark is the biggest predatory fish on the planet. It cruises the oceans, bursting into a high-speed chase to catch its prey.

Bigeye tuna
These tuna swim in deep, cold water using their big eyes to see in low light.

Pacific Ocean

The ocean is a large body of salt water that covers almost three quarters of the Earth's surface. The ocean is typically divided into five regions: the Pacific Ocean, the Atlantic Ocean, the Indian Ocean, the Arctic Ocean, and the Southern Ocean. The Pacific Ocean is the largest of the five regions.

Mako shark
This speedy swimmer is the fastest shark on Earth. It shoots through the water beneath its prey before twisting upward to surprise it. It can also jump 30 ft (9 m) out of the water!

Loggerhead sea turtle
The loggerhead sea turtle is the largest hard-shelled sea turtle in the world. Their large head and strong jaws give them their name.

Did you find them all?

Bioluminescent lanternfish
These deep-sea fish produce their own light. Their heads, stomachs, and tails glow in blue-green. This attracts smaller fish for them to eat.

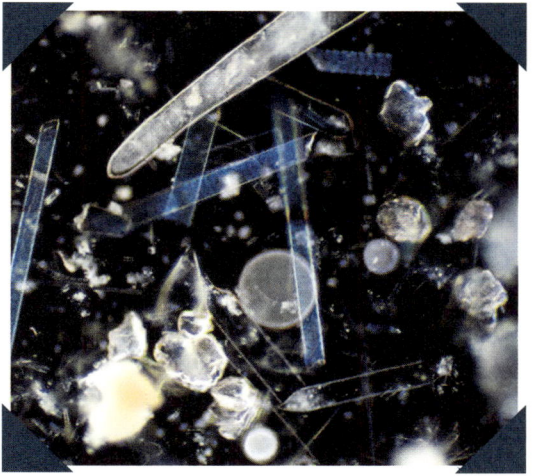

After 20 years of talks, a historic new treaty, called the UN High Seas Treaty, has been signed. These waters are threatened by climate change, pollution, and overfishing. Countries must work hard to ensure that the UN High Seas Treaty does protect our deep blue seas and the migratory species that depend on them too.

The people helping

The Schmidt Ocean Institute led a voyage to the White Shark Café to try to understand why these huge animals gather in the middle of the ocean when it seems to be empty. Scientists have tagged the sharks so that they can follow their movements and study their behavior.

Phytoplankton
These microscopic ocean plants photosynthesize to create half of all the oxygen we breathe.

Strawberry squid
This squid has lopsided eyes. A big one looks up, and a smaller eye looks down to the sea floor.

How you can help

Shark products can be found in food, shoes, and beauty supplies. To be sure you are not supporting the cruel trade in shark products, avoid products that contain shark liver oil or an ingredient called squalene.

Sperm whale
Sperm whales sleep hanging vertically in the water, gently bobbing with the swell.

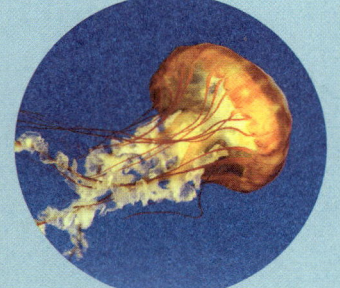

Medusa jellyfish
The medusa jellyfish is one of the few species benefiting from climate change. Their numbers are soaring because jellyfish thrive in warmer oceans and their predators are being overfished.

Ocean sunfish
These big, heavy, round fish look like a huge head. They lay an incredible 300,000,000 eggs at a time—more than any other vertebrate on Earth!

The Okavango Delta

It's the dry season, and most of Southern Africa is baking in the midday sun. But here in Botswana, cool waters are rushing to transform one of the world's biggest deserts into a sparkling oasis. As rainwater bursting from rivers surges across the Okavango Delta, this huge wetland explodes with life. Hippos begin to paddle through criss-crossing waterways, honking and grunting. Elephant families arrive after long migrations to splash through lily pad-covered lagoons, while lions get their paws wet, hungrily eyeing up grazing buffalo herds. Every year, this delta becomes crowded with animals drinking, playing, and soaking in these precious floods. Many endangered species rely on this jewel in the desert to survive.

Habitat

The Okavango Delta changes dramatically with the seasons. It floods every year with water from two rivers. The Okavango is a rare inland delta, because its waters never reach the sea.

The Okavango Delta landscape is made up of thousands of islands in a vast wetland. Migrating animals and birds make long journeys to reach the food-rich region.

Transition zone
Wetlands have characteristics of both dry land and underwater environments

African wild dog
African wild dogs are one of the most endangered mammals on Earth.

Lion
In the Okavango, lions have learned to hunt in water. This is the only place in the world where these big cats leap through water to surprise their prey.

Hippopotamus
Hippos have been given the nickname "river horses," because they love to wallow in rivers during the day to keep cool under the scorching sun.

Wetlands

A wetland is an area of land that is covered with water for at least part of the year. The water in wetlands can come from the ground, a river or lake, or the sea. A delta—like the Okavango Delta—is a type of wetland.

African elephant
Elephants are ecosystem engineers, which means that their actions change the landscape. They tear down trees and clear pathways as they move, which other animals can then use.

Did you find them all?

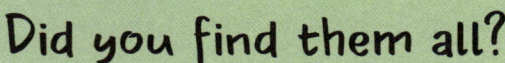

Termites
The Okavango's islands are mostly made by termites—billions of tiny insects building skyscraper homes. Trees grow on their muddy mounds, creating shade for lounging leopards and nesting spots for the Delta's birds.

African bullfrog

In spring, male African bullfrogs sing. This attracts females for mating but also warns rivals to stay away!

The people helping

The National Geographic Okavango Wilderness Project is mapping this landscape of wetlands and exploring its amazing biodiversity. The team behind the Okavango Delta project are now involving scientists and local communities in recording, monitoring, and protecting this precious place.

As global temperatures increase, the waters of the Okavango Delta will evaporate faster under an ever-warmer African sun. The rivers pouring into the Delta are also under threat. Businesses and cities upstream are taking more of this river water and polluting floodwaters that the Delta relies on.

Black rhino

Black rhinos were once extinct in the Okavango Delta. But they have been transported from South African parks and reintroduced here.

Red lechwe

These water-loving antelope are well adapted to their marshy home. They have powerful back legs and splayed hooves, which help them move quickly to escape predators.

Pel's fishing owl

The Pel's fishing owl is rare and difficult to spot, hiding in trees as it watches the water for fish. It dives silently into the Delta's cool waters at night to feed. Its haunting calls before dawn have been said to sound like a person shouting for help in a well!

How you can help

Look locally to find your closest wetland. It could be a pond, a river, or a marsh. Learn about the wildlife that call these wetlands home, and ask your school to celebrate World Wetlands Day on February 2.

Lily-trotter

The male lily-trotter scoops up his chicks and tucks them up under his wings. He then strides off, and the chicks' little legs can be seen dangling from under his feathers.

Nile monitor

The Nile monitor is Africa's longest lizard. It sunbathes on rocks and lurks in the reeds. It flicks out its long forked tongue, using it to follow the scent of its prey, before sneaking up on a wading bird's nest to steal an egg.

Sussex

In underwater forests around the world, kelp can be found gently swaying. Here, off the coast of England, the rocky crevices on the ocean floor where the kelp are tightly anchored are teeming with sea life. Weaving through shifting, secret spaces among the kelp's velvety blades are seals, cuttlefish, sharks, and even dolphins. The tentacles of an octopus disappear into dark shadows, and seals twist up through the seaweed curtain toward the water's surface for a breath of air. While wary shoals of fish dart around, a tiny, upright seahorse bobs along slowly. She's the slowest fish in these waters, and she's in no hurry today.

Can you find them all?

- Conger eel
- Cuttlefish eggs
- Catshark

Habitat

Kelp needs sun to grow, and so its blades stretch upward to the water's surface. Far below, it is stuck to the rocks with a holdfast which anchors this giant brown algae to the seabed.

Kelp creates dense forests offering lots of hidden homes for marine life. In Sussex, fish slip through this rippling underwater jungle, small snails graze along the kelp's floating leaves, and squid and sharks seek secret spaces to safely lay their eggs.

Landmass
Channels separate two landmasses that are close together, like England and France

Common cuttlefish
Cuttlefish can very quickly change their skin color to camouflage themselves while stalking their prey.

European bass
European bass spawn their eggs in batches. The eggs then float in the sea before hatching between three and four days later.

Channel

Kelp forests once stretched for hundreds of sq km in the English Channel. Channels are waterways between two bodies of land that are close to each other. Channels can be created naturally by glaciers or man-made. The English Channel is a naturally formed channel.

Gray seal
Seals use their streamlined bodies to twist and turn through the slippery kelp, searching for their favorite prey.

Spider crab
All sorts of tiny creatures make their home on the spider crab's pear-shaped, spiky shell. This camouflage helps hide it from its prey.

Did you find them all?

Conger eel
The conger eel can grow up to 9 ft 10 in (3 m) in length, and it is the biggest eel species in UK waters. These nocturnal eels spend their days hiding in rocks and come out at night to hunt.

Dolphin

Dolphins surf the swell above the kelp close to the water's edge, hunting for fish and squid.

The people helping

Blue Marine Foundation and Sussex Wildlife Trust are working with local communities, fishers, and scientists to help kelp forests recover along the UK's south coast. After trawling close to the shore was banned, the kelp's recovery and regrowth is being monitored and the impact recorded.

Kelp forests store the sun's energy as they grow, locking up carbon that helps the planet's battle against climate change. With protection from damaging fishing practices such as trawling, kelp—and the many marine creatures that depend on it—will return and restore nature's ocean balance.

Rare short-snouted seahorse

Seahorses are actually fish but are poor swimmers. They bob along slowly, sucking up their prey, and sometimes use their tail to cling onto the kelp's waving blades.

How you can help

Litter can be washed into the ocean from land, threatening all marine life. Join an organized litter-picking event to help stop trash from reaching the sea.

Sugar kelp

The parts of kelp that look like leaves are called "fronds." Sugar kelp has only one long, crinkly frond growing from its stem.

Common lobster

Not only are common lobsters blue on the outside, but they're blue on the inside too! Like snails and spiders, lobsters have blue blood.

Cuttlefish eggs

Cuttlefish eggs contain a very small amount of ink which makes them black, and they are grouped together in bunches. They're often called "sea grapes," as they look like the fruit.

Catshark

This spotty predator lays leathery egg cases called "mermaid's purses" which stick to the kelp. Sometimes they break off in a storm and get washed up on the beach.

Chambal River

In India's Chambal River, baby crocodiles clamber onto the back of a giant male. He's almost completely submerged under the surface, floating steadily in the deep, calm waters. On the sides of his head, huge eyes roll slowly backward and forward on the lookout for danger. His midriver crèche is tempting to the large wading birds that also call the Chambal River home. The braver babies take a dip close by—there's not enough room on board for everyone—their little snouts sticking straight up out of the water. They'll have the best spot when the scorching heat of India's midday sun beams down.

Can you find them all?

- Indian wolf
- Red-crowned roofed turtle
- Smooth-coated otter

Habitat

The wide Chambal River winds through central India. The National Chambal Sanctuary that stretches along this remote watery habitat protects the area, which is home to the world's largest population of the endangered gharial.

Watersheds

Different tributaries carry snowmelt and runoff from different areas

The Chambal is a clean river, rich in freshwater wildlife. Land animals like tigers and wolves that live in the vast scrublands beyond the river visit its sandy riverbanks to drink.

Ruddy shelduck

This little duck is mostly nocturnal, nibbling on water plants in the shallows at night. It also swims out to deeper waters to dip downward to feed, but it can't dive.

Mainstem

The larger river the tributary empties into is called the mainstem

Tributaries

Rivers are bodies of freshwater that flow downhill. Freshwater contains less than 1 percent salt. The starting point of a river is called the headwater and at the end is its mouth, where the river flows into a larger body of water, such as the ocean.

Gharial

The gharial is a long-nosed crocodile that can grow up to 19 ft 8 in (6 m) in length. Despite its large size, it is harmless to humans and only eats fish.

Sarus crane

This large crane is the tallest flying bird in the world, and it can grow up to 5 ft 11 in (1.8 m) tall.

Indian leopard

Known as the "rock leopards of Chambal," these big cats prefer life on steep river cliffs rather than the scrub and grassland leopards usually patrol.

Did you find them all?

Indian wolf

The Indian gray wolf has a speckled coat, which helps camouflage it against the landscape and makes it more difficult to spot. Its fur is thinner and shorter than other wolf species because of the warmer climate here.

Gangetic dolphin

This freshwater dolphin is almost completely blind. It uses sound waves to find its prey in the deep river pools where it prefers to feed.

The people helping

A team at the Gharial Ecology Project are studying these lumpy-nosed crocodiles. As part of their work, they tag gharials to track and record their behavior. They also visit local schools to share their experiences of this very special crocodile.

The banks of the Chambal River are home to more gharials than anywhere else in the world. Here, they lay their eggs and hatch their young. But the riverbanks are slowly disappearing. Illegal sand mining removes sand from beaches and rivers and uses it to make building materials, destroying the habitat the gharials rely on.

Indian skimmer

Indian skimmers keep themselves safe by nesting on midriver islands beyond the reach of jackals and other land predators.

Black-necked stork

To impress a mate, both male and female black-necked storks perform a dance, extending and fluttering their wings in an elegant display.

Marsh crocodile

Unlike the gharial, who swipes its prey, marsh crocodiles like to snap their jaws around large prey like deer or local livestock.

How you can help

The Chambal is a clean river, but many rivers are polluted by sewage. When you flush the toilet, the water is taken away to a sewage plant and cleaned before it is released into a river or the sea. Sometimes, the treatment plant does not remove things that have been thrown down the toilet, and these end up in our waterways. So remember the three Ps of what goes in the toilet: pee, poop, and (toilet) paper.

Red-crowned roofed turtle

This colorful freshwater turtle is found in deep rivers like the Chambal. Unlike most other freshwater turtles, they are vegetarian and graze on underwater algae.

Smooth-coated otter

These sleek river creatures hunt in a group. They swim upstream together in a V-shape to trap fish. When they catch a large fish, they use their strong webbed feet to haul it ashore to eat.

Can you find them all?

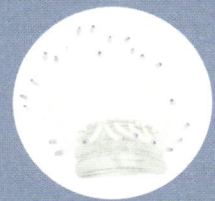

White sea anemone

Sea butterfly

Yellow sea lily

The Endurance shipwreck

For more than a hundred years, this ghostly shipwreck has rested on the seabed of the icy Antarctic Ocean. A colossal squid pulses in the dark, and the arms of starfish and sea anemones stretch into freezing waters, brushing past the ship's hull. Here, in the most remote ocean on Earth, the silence is broken only by whale song, as humpback calls echo hauntingly. Once, this ship—named *Endurance*—teemed with a different kind of life. Sailors sang shanties, a cat meowed, dogs barked, and explorers talked of adventures. But then disaster struck. *Endurance* became stuck in ice, and the crew were forced to abandon it as it slowly sank. Over time, the ship has become a deep-sea habitat, home to incredible and mysterious aquatic life.

The habitat

The Weddell Sea is part of the Antarctic Ocean. Much of the southern part of this sea is a permanent ice shelf. The darkness and crushing pressure mean that all life must adapt to survive in this extreme environment.

The life forms that live on or slip past *Endurance* grow and move very slowly—or not at all! At more than 9,840 ft (3,000 m) deep, this watery habitat is too cold for speed. Yet, scientists are amazed to discover plenty of life in this icy deep.

Weddell seal

Weddell seals can hold their breath underwater for more than an hour while looking out for breathing holes in the ice above!

Antarctic silverfish

Penguins, whales, and seals all chase this little silver fish. They can live for up to 10 years in very cold water—if they get the chance!

Colossal squid

Colossal squid fight with sperm whales. No one has ever seen this silent, deadly battle, but the squid's tentacles have been found in sperm whales' stomachs.

• Water
The Weddell Sea has the clearest water of any sea

The Weddell Sea

The Weddell Sea was originally called the George IV Sea. In 1900, it was renamed the Weddell Sea after the man who discovered it: James Weddell.

Minke whale

Minke whales seek shelter below the ice, and scientists use special underwater recorders to track their "quacking" call.

Did you find them all?

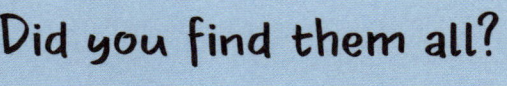

White sea anemone

This huge white anemone was found at the wheel of the *Endurance* shipwreck. Its sticky arms wave in the cold water, waiting to catch zooplankton floating by.

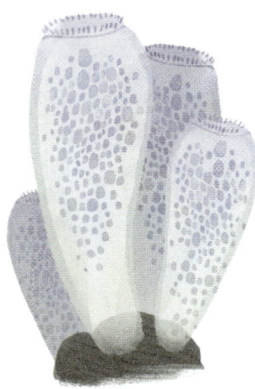

Glass sponge
Their basketlike cavities provide homes and cold-water nurseries for fish eggs and tiny deep-sea creatures looking for shelter.

Sea squirt
Sea squirts feed on tiny bits of dead things and poop—called "marine snow"—that float down to the bottom of the ocean.

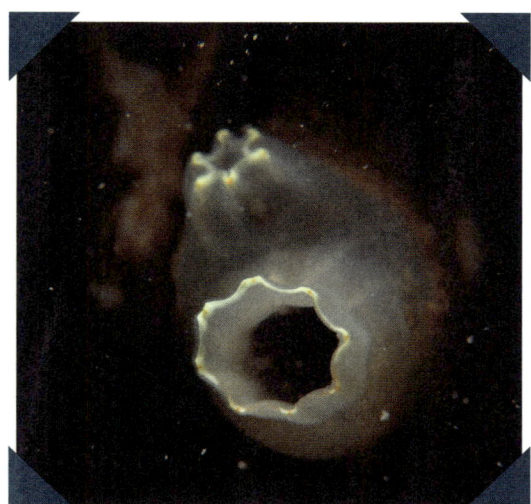

Krill
Krill are the main food of penguins, seabirds, and whales, who gulp down giant mouthfuls of these shrimplike creatures.

Squat lobster
Squat lobsters had never been found before in the Weddell Sea, until one was spotted scuttling across the *Endurance* shipwreck.

Sea star
These predators of the deep slide their stomach out of their mouth and lay it on top of their prey to slowly eat up!

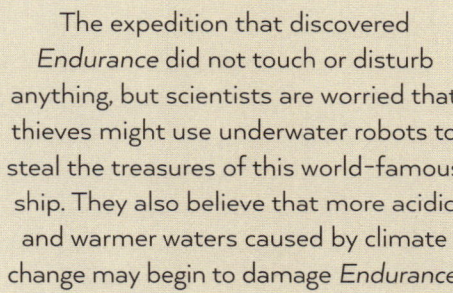

The expedition that discovered *Endurance* did not touch or disturb anything, but scientists are worried that thieves might use underwater robots to steal the treasures of this world-famous ship. They also believe that more acidic and warmer waters caused by climate change may begin to damage *Endurance*.

The people helping
The shipwreck of *Endurance* was found in 2021—more than 100 years after it sank—by the Falklands Maritime Heritage Trust, who were on an Antarctic expedition led by marine archaeologist, Mensun Bound. The ship was discovered using remote-controlled robots with underwater cameras.

How you can help
Water is a precious resource, and we should reuse it whenever we can. Leave a bucket outside to collect rainwater and then use the rainwater to give thirsty indoor plants a drink. This helps save money *and* the environment!

Sea butterfly
The sea butterfly is a tiny marine snail that grows to just 0.4 in (1 cm) in length. They catch the sea plankton they eat using a mucous web like a net. This net is 2 in (5 cm) long; much bigger than the sea butterfly itself.

Yellow sea lily
The bright yellow of this sea lily looks like a plant, but it is actually an ancient species of deep-sea animal that has been on Earth for approximately 480 million years!

The Amazon rainforest

It's the wet season in the Amazon, and rain is pouring down through the forest canopy. Huge drops of water trickle down the bark of towering trees and splash through a dense patchwork of leaves. The rain soaks the lush vegetation, filling every gap and hole. On the forest floor, a slippery frog is preparing to head up a tall tree. At first glance, it looks like she's covered in soft warts, but these jellylike blobs are actually her young. This poison dart frog is a good parent. She will drop her tadpoles into pools of rainwater that have gathered between the fleshy leaves of bromeliad plants. There, with plenty of prey, they will grow into froglets and eventually hop away from their waterlogged home.

Habitat

Some species spend part of their lifecycle in tiny freshwater habitats. Other larger species—like spiders and scorpions—visit to drink or stop by to feed.

Conditions

The amount of water and its temperature influence the animals that can use aquatic micro-habitats

Aquatic microhabitats

When rainwater collects in tree holes and brightly colored bromeliads, it creates microhabitats full of life. Microhabitats are small, and differ from the surrounding habitat. Aquatic microhabitats are typically cooler than the air around them and so can provide shelter in hot climates.

Aquatic microhabitats change with the seasons, filling up and drying out. In tropical forests, the leaf rosettes of plants called tank bromeliads can hold up to 704 fl oz (20 liters) of water and provide important habitats for life.

Jumping spider

Jumping spiders live and breed in bromeliads. Their poop contains nutrients that help bromeliads grow!

Polka-dot tree frog

Polka-dot tree frogs are naturally fluorescent. Under UV light, they glow bright green!

Climbing salamander

These salamanders produce toxins that can paralyze or even kill the salamander's main predator: snakes.

Strawberry poison frog

These little frogs lay their eggs on leaves and then take their young one by one and drop them into bromeliad pools where they grow into tadpoles.

Did you find them all?

Mosquito larvae

Some mosquitoes lay their eggs in bromeliad pools. The eggs hatch, and the larvae feed off nutrients in the still water before eventually turning into a flying mosquito and leaving the bromeliad pool.

Bromeliads

There are lots of different species of bromeliads, but one of the best known is the pineapple.

Bromeliad plants are popular with frogs. These humid homes shelter them from predators and provide food and water to drink. But frogs are in trouble. Of all the biodiversity on Earth, amphibians are at the greatest risk of extinction, especially in tropical forests. As the Amazon rainforest is cleared, frogs and salamanders face losing their homes. Deadly fungal skin diseases also threaten their survival.

The people helping

Scientists working with the Sustainable Amazon Network are helping reduce the impact of fires in the Amazon rainforest by creating firebreaks. Firebreaks help stop wildfires from destroying forests and killing the animals that live there.

Glittering-throated emerald hummingbird

The tiny wings of hummingbirds can beat up to 80 times per second as they hover to feed.

Glass frog

Glass frogs are transparent. You can see their blood pumping around their bodies and all of their internal organs through their skin.

Amazon whipsnake

Amazon whipsnakes can be found on both the ground and in the forest canopy. They have been known to slither around bromeliads looking for frogs to eat.

How you can help

Bromeliads can often be found in rainforests, but they can be grown closer to home too. Why not choose one suitable for the climate you live in, and plant a bright bromeliad in your own garden for frogs, birds, and small insects to use?

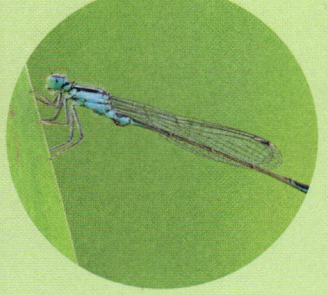

Damselfly

These elegant, winged insects are predators in bromeliad pools. In their early lifecycle, they live in the water and eat microscopic prey. As adults, they eat flies, larvae, and mosquitoes.

Diving beetle

Diving beetles eat damselfly larvae that live in tropical bromeliad pools. The diving beetles grab their prey with sharp pincers and holds it tightly between their front legs while taking a bite.

Can you find them all?

Atlantic blue tang

Flying fish

Yellowfin tuna

Ascension Island

A huge green sea turtle breaks through the rolling surf of the Atlantic Ocean onto the sand of a tiny, windy island. She isn't alone, as thousands like her will make this same pilgrimage from their feeding grounds off the coast of Brazil to Ascension Island. After weeks spent mating in the waters around the island, this female drags herself up to the beach. Sighing with exhaustion, she flicks away sand and begins to dig a hole. Under the cloak of night, she lays her eggs before quickly burying them to protect them from the island's predators who are on the hunt for a quick and easy meal. But there's no rest for the green sea turtle. Soon, she'll be on her way back to her faraway feeding grounds before returning here to lay more eggs once again.

Habitat

Ascension Island is the tip of a huge underwater volcano that rises from the sea. On land, colorful volcanic rocks bake in the sun, and Ascension Island's highest slopes are covered by one of the biggest man-made forests in the world.

Ascension Island is part of the Mid-Atlantic Ridge, the longest underwater mountain range on the planet. The deep waters that surround this oceanic island teem with unique sea life both big and small.

High islands
Oceanic islands are known as "high islands" regardless of how tall they actually are

Sooty tern
These elegant birds are known as "wide-awake birds" because of their constant chattering all day and night!

Sixgill shark
The sixgill shark is one of the ocean's largest predators, but it is rarely seen. It prefers to slip through the depths of the water, and so it is difficult to find and study.

Oceanic islands

When volcanoes on the ocean floor erupt, layers of lava build up and break through the surface of the water to form oceanic islands. Ascension Island is a volcano that broke through the ocean's surface around one million years ago.

Blue marlin
Some of the biggest blue marlin in the world speed around Ascension Island. Their streamlined bodies glint in shiny colors from blue to black and silver gray.

Ascension spurge

Ascension spurge is endemic to Ascension Island. It is critically endangered, as other non-native plants have stifled its growth.

Did you find them all?

Atlantic blue tang
Despite their name, the blue tang fish isn't always blue. Younger fish are yellow. As adults, the Atlantic blue tang's color can change, for example, to show that they are feeling stressed.

Procaris ascensionis
This white shrimp darts around small saltwater rock pools on Ascension Island—their only home in the world.

The people helping
Conservationists working with Blue Marine Foundation are monitoring sea turtles as they crawl up Ascension Island's beaches to make their nests. The conservation workers collect data about the size of the turtles and the number of eggs they lay to learn more about them. Conservationists also free turtles that are stuck and help them get back to the water.

Green sea turtle
Each year, the island's beaches are churned up by green sea turtles digging nest holes. Their criss-crossed tracks can be seen on the sand.

In the past, the ocean life around Ascension Island was destroyed by giant tuna fishing fleets that also caught turtles, sharks, and seabirds by mistake. But in 2019, the largest marine reserve in the Atlantic was created around the island. By banning fishing, it has been possible to restore the island's spectacular marine life.

Ascension frigatebird
On land, male frigatebirds puff out their big red throat pouch to attract a mate. At sea, these jet-black birds feast on flying fish that jump out of the water.

Resplendent pygmy angelfish
These fish are endemic to Ascension Island. They are born neither male nor female and can change sex during their life, depending on the mating needs of the population.

How you can help
The number of green sea turtles on Ascension Island has increased after humans stopped harvesting them for meat. Share this conservation success story with your friends and family, or write about it for a school project. When people work together to protect endangered species around the world, incredible things are possible!

Flying fish
These fish have wings and can leap out of the ocean to glide in the air. They do this to escape predators but can be unlucky if a seabird swoops low to snatch them as an easy meal.

Yellowfin tuna
This top ocean predator is migratory. It swims in huge schools, often joining other tuna fish, dolphins, and even whales on their journeys.

Lake Titicaca

As the sun sets on the Andes mountains, the temperature begins to drop. In the depths of Lake Titicaca, underwater giants start to stir. With long, powerful back legs, giant frogs push off from the lake floor. Their baggy and wrinkled skin hangs off their bodies and flaps around like a cloak as they kick forward through the weeds. As darkness falls, they rise from the mud to hunt, their wide eyes searching for prey. In these murky depths, tiny fish dart around broken pottery and snails crawl along the ruins of the temple of an ancient civilization lost to the lake long ago.

Can you find them all?

Karachi fish   Titicaca grebe   Heleobia

Habitat

Lake Titicaca is an ancient lake that has held water for more than a million years. It is also the highest lake in South America. The sun's rays are fierce here, and strong winds whip across its huge surface.

Turnover
Lake water moves around seasonally as waters of different temperatures mix

The lake is fed by 27 rivers. Only the Desaguadero River flows out. But under intense sun at this altitude, most water just evaporates into the thin air. The lake never freezes, so today's man-made island homes float on its surface all year.

Lake Titicaca giant frog
This is the world's largest fully aquatic frog, and it grows up to 7.9 in (20 cm) long. Its baggy skin helps it absorb more oxygen, which it needs in this high-altitude air.

Andean geese
Male Andean geese have high, whistling calls, but the females make low, grunting sounds.

Lakes

Lakes are large bodies of slow-moving or still water that are surrounded by land. Their water comes from snow, rain, melting ice, and groundwater. When water leaves a lake by a river or other similar outlet, it is an open lake. If water leaves a lake only through evaporation, it is called a closed lake.

Totora
The totora plant is incredibly strong. On Lake Titicaca, the Uru people use totora to build the floating islands they live on. Elsewhere, it is used for thatch and to make small fishing boats.

Catfish
Catfish have whiskers like cats that are covered in sensors. Because they have small eyes, they use their whiskers to feel around and "taste" prey in murky waters.

Did you find them all?

Karachi fish
These tiny finger-length fish have small, round yellow and black bodies. They can often be found nibbling algae near the surface of the lake. They are called "annual fish" because they only live for a year.

The people helping

The Lake Titicaca water frog is now critically endangered after many years of being poached and the lake's waters being polluted. Local women make frog-themed crafts—such as puppets, toys, and beanies—which they sell on the shore of the lake. They share the story of the water frog with customers to encourage its protection.

Vicuña
This delicate, fleecy animal is part of the camel family that also includes llamas and alpacas. Females live together in a group with a single male who acts as a protector.

Many of the species found here can't be found anywhere else on Earth. But the lake's water levels are falling as glaciers shrink and rain patterns change with global climate change. The lake is also polluted by cities on its shores and the giant baggy frog that calls this place home is threatened by poaching.

Wild guinea pig
Wild guinea pigs can run as fast as 19 ft 8 in (6 m) per second and leap as high as 1 ft 12 in (60 cm).

Many-colored rush tyrant
In Spanish, this bird has been nicknamed *siete colores*, which means "seven colors" because of its bright feathers.

Rainbow trout
Rainbow trout were brought from North America to Lake Titicaca in the 1930s so that people living on its shores would have more to eat. But trout is an invasive species, and it eats the food of local fish, which has caused their numbers to decline.

How you can help

When leaves from trees fall and start to decompose, they release phosphorus. If phosphorus mixes with rainwater and gets carried into rivers and lakes it causes more algae to grow, which blocks out sunlight. This can threaten underwater plants and animals that need sunlight to survive. So when the seasons change, take some time to sweep up the leaves from your driveway or patio.

Titicaca grebe
The main population of this endangered duck lives on Lake Titicaca. Titicaca grebes do not fly, but if they face danger, they paddle fast toward open water on the lake rather than hiding in the weeds.

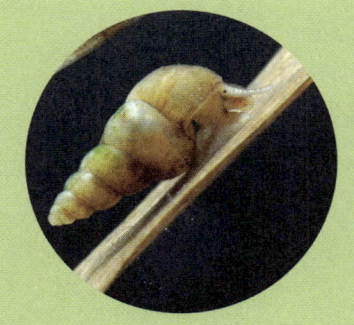

Heleobia
Snails cannot hear predators because they don't have ears, but they have an amazing sense of smell that is better than a human's. This helps them find food yards away.

The Galápagos Islands

Against the grays and blacks of the rocky shore, the rainbow skin of a Christmas iguana is hard to miss. It's mating season for this dinosaurlike creature in the Galápagos Islands, and his scaly skin has brightened from black to festive greens and reds to attract a mate. After deep diving into the ocean to feed on algae, he emerges from the water, snorting to clear his nostrils. As he does, Sally Lightfoot crabs scuttle across his back, cleaning ticks from the iguana's scaly skin. Now, this colorful lizard must jostle for space on the rocks. Eventually, he finds himself a spot to take a break and catch some sun.

Habitat

The Galápagos Islands are volcanic islands in the Pacific Ocean. Their peaks rise from tropical seas with coral reefs and shallow lagoons. Sandy shores, green grasses, and cacti spread over patches of this rocky land.

Fragmentation
Islands of an archipelago that have separated from a larger landmass are called continental fragments

Beyond land, the Pacific Ocean teems with marine life on the move. These islands lie in an important migratory corridor for sharks, manta rays, sea turtles, and whales swimming between Ecuador and Costa Rican waters.

Marine iguana
When marine iguanas get into the ocean, their heartbeat slows right down. This means they can use less energy and look for food for longer.

Large painted locust
Large painted locusts can be found on all the Galápagos Islands, except Española.

Archipelago
A group of islands closely arranged in a body of water is known as an archipelago. The body of water can be a lake, river, or ocean. Most archipelago islands are formed by volcanoes erupting from the floor of the ocean. Archipelagos can be found all over the world, from Japan to Finland.

Red-lipped batfish
The red-lipped batfish fish uses its fins like legs to walk on to find prey.

Whitetip reef shark
During the day, whitetip reef sharks stack themselves on top of each other in caves and only come out to hunt at night.

Did you find them all?

Sally Lightfoot crab
These agile, jumping crabs can run in four different directions and scale vertical rocky slopes, which helps them avoid predators. They scavenge whatever they find on the beach to eat, helping keep beaches clean.

Blue-footed booby

The male blue-footed booby struts around showing off his bright blue feet as part of his mating ritual. Bluer feet = more attractive.

The Galápagos Islands lie in the middle of the Pacific Ocean. They are part of a Mega-Marine Reserve. It is the first time a fishing-free swimway has been declared to create a safe corridor to protect migratory species.

Galápagos penguin

The Galápagos penguin is the only penguin to live north of the equator. When they're hot, they pant to cool down—like a dog!

The people helping

The Galápagos Conservation Trust is helping families in the Galápagos Islands grow their own food and endemic plants. Local communities are now more connected with the flora of the islands and committed to protecting it.

Prickly pear cactus

Tall cacti are found on the Galápagos Islands where tortoises live. Shorter cacti can be found on the islands that are a tortoise-free zone.

Ocean sunfish

Sunfish earned their name by hanging out close to the ocean's surface to soak up the sun.

How you can help

After a day at the beach, don't forget to ruin your sandcastle. While they're fun to build and show off, they can be very difficult for young sea turtles and tortoises to navigate around. They can also make it more difficult for sea turtles to find a safe place to lay their eggs.

Galápagos lava lizard

Galápagos lava lizards can often be seen performing push-ups. They do this to appear stronger and to put off other male lava lizards who may be tempted to fight them.

Lava heron

Camouflaged against the gray rock, this little heron wades along the seashore looking for small fish and crabs. When they spot their prey, they swiftly stab it with their razor-sharp beak.

Namibian Islands' Marine Protected Area

The delicate dancing of Namibia's flamingos is shrouded in a blanket of early morning sea mist. On this vast coastline where the desert meets the ocean, flamingos bow and raise their necks, slurping shrimp in sheltered lagoons. They shimmy in flocks across these clear, salty shallows, daintily lifting their spindly legs. Honking and chattering in endlessly shifting crowds, they are an elegant spectacle in pink. Farther out, black and white orcas surf the rough swell. In contrast to the gentle feasting in the lagoons, they are pursuing their prey in organized packs. From the sand where they're relaxing, fur seals survey the scene.

Habitat

The coastline of Namibia is dotted with underwater mountains and tiny islands. They were given names including Plumpudding Island, Christmas Island, and Roastbeef Island by hungry sailors who were passing by long ago!

Sea levels
Rising sea levels can flood lagoons

The Benguela Current is a sea current that runs along the length of the Namibian coast. It pushes nutrients from the deep sea closer to the surface. This supports African penguins, flocks of flamingos, dolphins, whales, and huge populations of seabirds.

Cape gannets
Cape gannets dive downward to snatch their fish prey. They can reach diving speeds of up to 62 mph (100 kph).

African penguin
African penguins are the only species of penguins on the African coast. They are clumsy land walkers but zoom about in the sea.

Lagoons

Lagoons are shallow waters that are protected from large bodies of water by barrier islands, coral reefs, or sandbars. The size and depth of coastal lagoons—like the ones found in Namibia—depends on the sea level. If the sea level is low, lagoons look more like wetlands. If the sea level is high, they look more like lakes.

Heaviside's dolphin
These small dolphins are only found in waters off the coast of Namibia, where the Benguela Current brings them plenty of food.

Southern fur seal
Namibia is home to the world's biggest colony of southern fur seals. Seal pups make a meowing noise like a cat!

Did you find them all?

Sardines
Sardines travel together in schools. They pack themselves tightly together in a ball-shaped formation called "bait balls" to make it harder for predators to snatch individual fish. These bait balls can even be seen above the water.

Lesser flamingo
A group of flamingos is called a flamboyance!

The Namibian Islands' MPA is the second-largest marine reserve in Africa. However, the wildlife living and migrating through this area are at risk from overfishing, marine diamond mining, pollution, and animal harvesting. This important marine reserve is currently not being patrolled, and better management is urgently needed to protect it.

The people helping

The Namibian Islands' Marine Protected Area (MPA) was designated as a protected site in 2009, but no plans for its conservation were ever agreed upon. Blue Marine Foundation and Namibia Nature Foundation are working with local groups to come up with a plan to manage the MPA.

Damara tern
When Damara terns are breeding, the top of their heads and their beaks are black. When they are not breeding, their foreheads turn white.

Southern right whale
The southern right whale is a curious creature who swims close to fishing and whale-watching boats.

Dusky dolphin
These dolphins gather in huge pods of up to 1,000 animals to hunt. They leap and whistle as they play in the water after feeding.

How you can help

If you eat fish, choose sustainably caught fish. Ask your fishmonger for fish that has been caught from smaller local boats closer to shore. This fishing method is less damaging to marine ecosystems.

Brine shrimp
These little crustaceans are an important food for flamingos. Brine shrimp contain a chemical called carotene—which is also found in carrots—that turns a flamingo's feathers pink!

Bank cormorant
This sleek bird fishes in tall brown seaweed close to the coast of Namibia. In these underwater kelp forests, the cormorant is on the lookout for lobsters, octopuses, and fish.

Antarctic ice shelves

Beneath the swells of deep Antarctic waters, billions of tiny pink creatures are on the move. Their feathery legs ripple along their bodies as they migrate from the ocean surface to the ocean floor and back, over and over. These krill swarm under the thick ice, trying to avoid the hungry blue whales all around. But it's no use. The pod of blue whales surge up again and again with wide-open mouths. Yet still, the icy waters squirm with krill, and what the whales didn't catch is now up for grabs. Twisting, circling seals scoop up thousands of krill in a single mouthful, and zooming emperor penguins are eager to make sure they don't miss out.

Habitat

The Southern Ocean surrounds the great frozen landmass of Antarctica. Here, sea ice forms when the ocean freezes. When this sea ice attaches to land, it becomes an ice shelf. Young krill graze on plankton and ice algae that live underneath the ice, turning it shades of green.

Temperature

The temperature of the water here varies between 50° F (10° C) and 28° F (-2° C)

The sea ice protects krill larvae from predators, but this shelter melts and expands over the seasons and is increasingly disappearing in warming seas. As this habitat changes, super-swarms of krill are shifting and shrinking, affecting animals that rely on them for a meal.

Leopard seal

Male leopard seals make a lot of underwater noise. They hang upside down and rock from side to side to warn other males to stay away or when calling for a mate.

Arctic tern

This little bird makes a record-breaking migration between the Earth's north and south poles. In its lifetime, the Arctic tern flies the equivalent of the distance from Earth to the moon and back—three times!

Southern Ocean

The Southern Ocean is the world's youngest ocean, as it was only formed 30 million years ago! It is the second smallest ocean on Earth and the coldest. Around 90 percent of the ice found on Earth is found in Antarctica and the Southern Ocean.

Snow petrel

Snow petrels are one of only three bird species that have ever been seen at the South Pole.

Antarctic toothfish

These fish produce special antifreeze chemicals in their bodies which help them survive in very cold, deep waters.

Did you find them all?

Giant Antarctic sea spider

This arthropod can reach the size of a small dog! The Antarctic sea spider has five pairs of legs. Because they have such small bodies, their vital organs can be found in their legs.

Emperor penguin

The biggest of the penguin species is the emperor penguin. They live in colonies of up to a million nesting pairs. In Antarctic winters—when temperatures drop to almost -94°F (-70°C)—they huddle together with their heads tucked in against bitter winds.

Antarctica is a pristine wilderness protected by the Antarctic Treaty. This international agreement is supported by lots of countries that work together to protect the continent. But as climate change warms the ocean, the sea ice shelves where krill feed are melting. Scientists believe that if climate change is not slowed down, only half of all the krill hatching today will survive.

Albatross

Albatrosses have the biggest wingspan of any bird. This helps these huge seabirds cover a distance of up to 500 miles (805 km) in a day.

The people helping

British Antarctic Survey (BAS) scientists are exploring this pristine environment to investigate how our climate is changing, how fast ice is melting, and how quickly sea levels are rising. They hope to learn more about how the balance of nature on Earth is affected by climate change. This will help humans make changes to reduce our impact on the planet.

Hoff crab

Hoff crabs are covered in bacteria that makes them look hairy.

Crocodile icefish

Crocodile icefish have colorless blood. This is because they don't have hemoglobin, which is the protein that makes blood red.

How you can help

You can help save Antarctica by changing your habits to slow down climate change. Walk or bike instead of traveling by car, especially for short journeys. Trees are also great for absorbing carbon dioxide from the air. More trees = less carbon dioxide, so find out how you can help plant trees where you are.

Whale barnacles

Whale barnacles attach themselves to the skin of a whale—the "host"— and hitch a ride. This makes it easier for the barnacles to filter food as their host glides through the ocean.

Macaroni penguin

Macaroni penguins share responsibility for incubating their eggs. The parents do it together at first and then take turns to protect the egg or hunt. The penguin left to incubate the egg will not eat while their mate is gone!

The Cave of the Hanging Snakes

In the Mexican jungle lies a deep limestone cave. During the day, the cave is silent and still, but as dusk falls, hundreds of hungry bats begin to stir. In the pitch black, the sound of leathery wings frenziedly flapping suddenly fills the air as bats swarm out into the night. But these creatures face an extraordinary challenge to survive, as this cave is also home to dozens of snakes... and they're hungry too. Darting out of dark crevices with open jaws, these blind and deaf yellow-red rat snakes strike. They clamp their prey, curling their long, heavy bodies around the bats. In the shallow waters below, fish, eels, and other crustaceans carry on about their business, oblivious to the midair feast happening above.

Can you find them all?

White lady fish

Albino crustacean

Brotula eel

Habitat

Known locally as Kantemó Cave, this cave is very unusual. The flooded underground cavern showcases how animals adapt to different habitats and opportunities to survive.

Formation
Caves can take thousands of years to form.

Permanent cave dwellers are called troglobites. Other animals—like bats, birds, and bears—use caves for shelter, and some elephants head into caves to lick salt from the rocks.

Mexican free-tailed bat
These bats have wrinkled skin around their mouths, which makes it easier for them to open it wide to catch their prey.

Swallows
As well as "The Cave of the Hanging Snakes," there is also a "Cave of Swallows" in Mexico. Every morning, the swallows fly up in circles from their overnight roosts deep below.

Caves

There are many different types of caves across the world. The way they are formed and where the water in them comes from depends on what type of cave they are. The most common type of cave is a karst cave. Rainwater mixes with carbon dioxide and begins to dissolve fractured rocks. Eventually, caves are formed.

Cave Molly
Cave Mollys are called "extremophiles," because they can exist in extreme conditions where most other life can't.

Hells Bells stalactite
Unusually, these huge bell-shaped stalactites grow underwater. Scientists believe they were formed in ancient times.

Did you find them all?

White lady fish
This small fish swims in freshwater caves without light. It doesn't have any eyeballs, and instead uses its chemical senses to hunt.

Mexican tetra fish

These fish use six different sounds to communicate. Those that live in dark caves make different sounds from the ones that live in light places, like rivers.

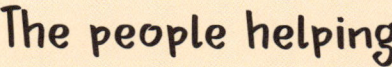

All over the world, damp, dark caves store water and create unique habitats, but these ecosystems are very fragile. Pollution of the water or small changes in light can threaten the unique life-forms that have evolved in caves over millions of years.

Mexican mealybug

Male mealybugs do not have a mouth, because the adults do not eat!

The people helping

Local people are proud to share their stories and knowledge of "The Cave of the Hanging Snakes." They lead visitors on guided tours of the cave so more people can learn about these snake-catching bats and the other creatures that call this place home.

Yellow-red rat snake

These nonvenomous snakes can grow more than 3 ft 3 in (1 m) long.

Oaxaca cave sleeper

This fish has no eyes. Over a long time, the species has adapted to an environment where eyes are no longer useful.

How you can help

It might be tempting to explore wild places on your own, but always join a guided tour when necessary and respect areas that are out of bounds. By doing so, you'll be helping protect habitats and the creatures who live there.

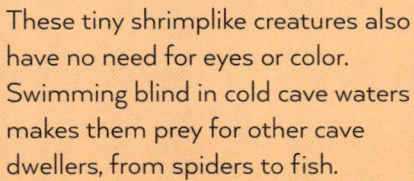

Albino crustacean

These tiny shrimplike creatures also have no need for eyes or color. Swimming blind in cold cave waters makes them prey for other cave dwellers, from spiders to fish.

Brotula eel

Brotulas can be found in deep and shallow waters as well as freshwater caves. Some brotulas have eyes, but those that live in the deep sea or caves are partially or completely blind.

Can you find them all?

Totoaba

Humboldt squid

Anchovies

The Sea of Cortez

Off the coast of sunny California, the smallest whale in the world gently surfs without a splash. While dolphins and rays swim and leap around him, this shy vaquita spends most of his time just beneath the surface of these warm waters. His pandalike eyes and dark, smiling lips are hidden from view as he takes a quiet breath. He's busy fishing, and he's not a fussy eater, grabbing squid, fish, and any other crunchy crustaceans he spots. As the little vaquita surfaces, the shadow of an enormous blue whale passes below. She's just one of the great whales migrating to the Sea of Cortez in spring to give birth and nurse her young.

Habitat

The Sea of Cortez, nicknamed "the aquarium of the world," supports a dazzling display of marine life, and its sheltered waters have massive plankton blooms providing plenty of food. The warm waters here welcome the hundreds of migrating leatherback turtles, sharks, seabirds, and whales that visit throughout the year.

Many species living in or close to the Sea of Cortez are found nowhere else on Earth. This biodiversity hotspot is fed by more than five rivers—including the great Colorado River—and has more than 37 volcanic islands dotting its deep blue waters.

Blue whale
Up to 300 blue whales gather in the Sea of Cortez each year after a long migration from colder northern waters. Here, they nurse their calves in these warm, sheltered waters.

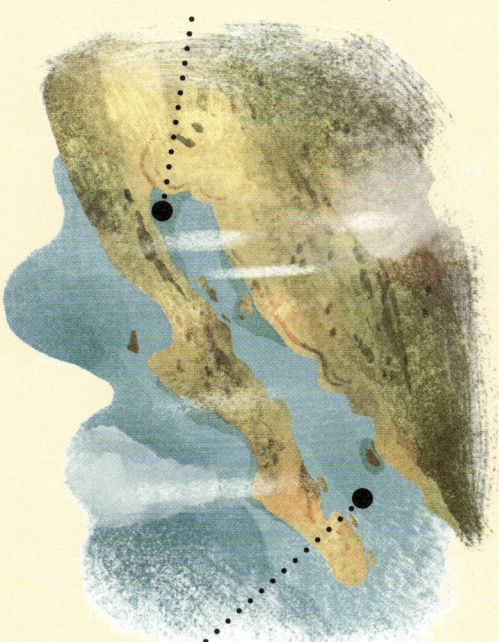

Inlet
The inlet is usually deeper than the inlet of a bay.

Hammerhead shark
The head of a hammerhead shark contains jelly-filled sensors that pick up electromagnetic signals from moving prey. This helps them hunt in dark, murky waters.

Brown pelican
This chocolate-colored bird plummets down into the sea to scoop up anchovies and other fish in the pouch hanging under their long beak.

Opening
The opening is typically narrower than the opening of a bay.

Gulfs

The Sea of Cortez is sometimes called the Gulf of California. A gulf is a part of the ocean that has penetrated land. Gulfs can be a variety of shapes, sizes, and depths, and they're usually found along the shores of continents.

Devil ray
The Sea of Cortez turns black with the annual arrival of thousands of devil rays. They leap elegantly up into the air but come down with a big belly splash.

Orca
Orcas are incredibly fast swimmers. They have been recorded traveling at speeds of more than 30 mph (48 kph)!

Did you find them all?

Anchovies
Huge shoals of anchovies dart around the Sea of Cortez. These tiny silver fish are an important food source for whales, sharks, dolphins, bigger fish, and people, too.

Vaquita

The vaquita whale was only discovered in 1958. Before that, it was believed to be a mythical creature!

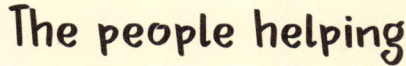

The people helping

Local communities have taken action to protect their future. They petitioned the government to protect the Sea of Cortez from overfishing and illegal fishing. The government agreed that management was needed, and local people now patrol these waters to keep poachers away.

The Sea of Cortez is protected by UNESCO, yet the vaquita is now dangerously close to extinction, and there are fewer than 20 left in the world. The fate of this little whale is linked to totoaba fish. Fishers lay huge nets to catch the totoaba fish, but they mistakenly tangle vaquitas too. This is known as by-catch.

California sea lion

Female sea lions and their pups have a unique scent and use unique vocalizations. This means a female sea lion can tell which pups are her own among hundreds of sea lion pups.

Leatherback sea turtle

The leatherback is the largest and most endangered of the seven sea turtle species. It can deep dive to more than 3,281 ft (1,000 m)—that's deeper than most marine mammals.

How you can help

The communities around the Sea of Cortez successfully convinced the government to protect this gulf. You have the power to do the same! Find out about a campaign close to you with a goal of protecting a local waterway and get involved.

Humboldt squid

Difficult to spot, this giant squid can change color and camouflage itself in its deepwater home. Its 10 suckered tentacles with barbed hooks stretch out to surprise and grab its prey.

Totoaba

This is a spectacular fish, which can grow to up to 6 ft 7 in (2 m) long. It is endemic to the Sea of Cortez, but it is extremely rare because it's illegally fished to be eaten as a delicacy in Chinese cuisine.

Jervis Bay

It's almost midnight in southeastern Australia. Waves gently roll onto the sandy beach of Jervis Bay, and the shoreline shimmers and glows a soft blue. Thousands of microscopic plankton are creating an incredible light display along the coast as far as the eye can see. Farther out in the water, the slippery gray of a pod of dolphins is just visible. With one eye always open, the dozing dolphins take a deep breath through their blowholes, gently rippling the water. Even farther out, great whales and sharks steer slowly through the blue deep, casting shadows. Far below the surface, luminous jellyfish, glowing snails, and deep-sea coral create magical flashes of neon in a spectacular underwater light show.

Habitat

Jervis Bay in southeast Australia is a white sandy beach with crystal clear waters. It is also one of several places on the planet where incredible ocean bioluminescence occurs along the shoreline a few times each year.

Borders
Land borders on three sides.

Bioluminescence is created by living things giving off light. In the ocean, many different animals make light, from fish and squid to jellyfish and plankton. In the ocean, bioluminescence is usually blue, because blue light travels most easily through water.

Indo-Pacific bottlenose dolphin
Indo-Pacific bottlenose dolphins are known to be very social. Females have lots of female friends, and males form strong bonds that can last their whole lives.

Hooded plover
Hooded plover chicks cannot fly for their first 35 days, so they look for food on the beach. If they hear their parents call out a predator alarm, the chicks know to run for cover.

Mouth
Where the bay opens to a lake or ocean.

Bays

Bays are bodies of water that are partially surrounded by land. Bays are normally smaller and not as enclosed as gulfs. They are sometimes called sounds or bights. The water in bays is usually brackish. This means that it is saltier than freshwater but not as salty as the ocean.

Flatback sea turtle
This species of sea turtle lives only in Australian waters. It has an unusual flat shell that is so soft that predators—such as sharks and saltwater crocodiles—can leave bite marks on it.

Did you find them all?

Southern spotlight loosejaw
This deep-sea dragonfish produces green and red lights from organs underneath its eyes. They help it find prey in the dark ocean where it lives.

White-faced storm petrel
White-faced storm petrels glide close to the water's surface and use their webbed feet to gather plankton to eat.

Jervis Bay is a marine park, which means it is protected for its wildlife as well as for the Wreck Bay Indigenous people. There are strict rules to control fishing and pollution that threaten the ocean.

The people helping
Conservation Volunteers Australia arrange events for local people to preserve Jervis Bay. Volunteers help remove sea spurge from the beaches around the bay. This toxic weed is invasive. It takes the place of native plants and prevents birds from using the beach for nesting.

Pilot whale
These whales are called pilot whales because it used to be believed that each pod had a leader, or a "pilot."

Gray nurse shark
When baby gray nurse sharks are born, they're already 3 ft 3 in (1 m) long. They are about 11 ft 6 in (3.5 m) long when fully grown.

False killer whale
False killer whales are actually dolphins. They swim together, sometimes in superpods of hundreds. They also hunt together and share their food, even with human divers!

How you can help
Avoid using single-use plastics. Sea turtles mistake plastic bags for food because they look like jellyfish, and seabirds and fish can get tangled in them. By using nonplastic alternatives and saying "no" to plastic bags, you will help save marine life.

Weedy seadragon
This little fish looks more like a floating weed. They are poor swimmers, drifting with the current in seagrass meadows, seaweed, and rocky reefs. They do not have any known predators.

Eastern blue devil fish
Despite the "devil" in their name, these electric blue fish are shy and harmless. They loiter alone in reef crevices and are most active at night.

The Maldives

In shade just below the water's surface, fish dart and weave their way through the chunky roots of mighty mangrove trees. In this great underwater forest, young fish, crabs, octopuses, and sharks find shelter among the twisted thickets. They're safe here from the ocean predators that are too big to swim into these tangled forests. A young, grumpy-mouthed grouper meanders slowly through the tangled root system. When he is older, he will leave this fish nursery and head out toward the coral. There, he will spawn in a group so big that he and his fellow groupers will block out the sun.

Can you find them all?

- Honeycomb moray eel
- Snake sea cucumber
- Guitarfish

Habitat

These mangrove forests connect to shallow lagoons and seagrass meadows stretching out toward coral reefs.

Tropical tree
Mangroves can only survive in temperatures above 66°F (19°C)

Flooded mangrove forests are critically important fish nurseries and also provide shelter for many other marine creatures.

Seagrass
Seagrass relies on light to grow. That's why it is only found in shallow waters.

Giant grouper
The giant grouper is a very accurate name for this huge fish. They can weigh more than 800 lb (360 kg)!

Roots
Partly exposed roots take in oxygen

Mangrove forests

Mangrove forests are very important for protecting the land from hurricanes and storms. There are approximately 40 species of mangrove tree. Mangroves used to cover much of the world's tropical and subtropical coastlines, but many have been lost to climate change.

Gray reef shark
During the day, gray reef sharks are sociable. They gather in groups of up to 20 on the edge of the reef. But at night, they set off alone to hunt.

Black mangrove
Black mangroves absorb saltwater from the ocean, use the water, and then discharge the salt. Salt crystals can sometimes be seen on the black mangrove's leaves.

Did you find them all?

Honeycomb moray eel
These eels spend the day hidden in rocky crevices but slip out at night to ambush prey. These deadly hunters may look like snakes, but they are actually fish.

Crown-of-thorns starfish

These starfish are an invasive species. They crawl over coral reefs, devouring the coral and killing huge areas of reef if they are allowed to get out of control.

Reef manta ray

When feeding in one place, reef manta rays roll over and over with their mouths open to catch as much plankton as they can.

Triton conch

This huge shell plays an important role in the coral reef, as it is one of the few animals that feeds on the crown-of-thorns starfish that is well known for destroying coral.

Mangroves and seagrass both store carbon in the ocean. Scientists believe that seagrass stores carbon 35 times faster than tropical forests! But seagrass is sometimes removed so that tourists can swim in clear waters. The Maldives Resilient Reefs Project is working to protect these habitats and keep the seagrass intact.

Humpback red snapper

In clear waters, dense schools of humpback red snappers spend their days just drifting together with the current. They only go their own way to feed at night.

The people helping

Blue Marine Foundation scientists have spent many hours diving in Maldivian waters to learn more about the grouper fish that spawn there. After many years of research, the local environment minister has been persuaded to protect this area to save the groupers.

How you can help

Climate change is the greatest threat to the planet. It causes ice caps to melt and sea levels to rise. Write to your local congressperson to ask what they are doing to fight climate change.

Snake sea cucumber

Giant sea cucumbers can grow up to 6 ft 7 in (2 m) long. They are found on sea floors around the world. They are poisonous to most would-be predators, so they can slither over the coral scavenging for food in peace.

Guitarfish

These fish with guitar-shaped heads bury themselves in the sand to eat worms, crabs, and clams. They are related to rays, and, like rays, they give birth to live young.

Caspian Sea

A large, whiskered fish glides slowly through the waters of the Caspian Sea. This beluga sturgeon is the size of a small bus, and she is at home in this gigantic saltwater lake. Her ancestors swam in seas all around the world at the same time as dinosaurs roamed the Earth. But today, most beluga sturgeons live here. Soon, she'll leave the Caspian Sea and swim a great distance up Russia's great Volga River, heading for the shallow gravel beds where she was born. Her amazing instincts drive her and other migrating fish upriver to lay their eggs. With her belly full and huge river dams blocking her path, it'll be a difficult journey, but she must do it for her species to survive.

Habitat

The Caspian Sea waters once flowed into the Atlantic and Pacific oceans. Today, this huge area of water is completely surrounded by land. But it is still salty, which shapes the lives of the creatures that live there, many of whom live nowhere else on Earth.

Rain
The source of water in endorheic basins is rainwater

In this dry, sandy landscape, shallow wetlands around the Caspian Sea shore are important resting and feeding places for migrating birds. Flamingos and swans fly in for winter, joining thousands of other birds seeking cool waters.

Caspian gull
Caspian gulls are usually migratory, but many settle around the Caspian Sea. They ward off rivals with a noisy call that sounds like a braying donkey!

Beluga sturgeon
The beluga sturgeon is the biggest of the seven species of sturgeon in the Caspian Sea. It uses its long whiskers to help it find prey.

Endorheic basin

The Caspian Sea is an example of an endorheic basin. Water does not flow out of endorheic basins. Instead, it is lost through geological rifts and natural phenomena, such as evaporation. When water evaporates, minerals—like salt—are left behind, making the water that remains even saltier.

Caspian tern
The Caspian tern is recognizable by its croaky call and razor-sharp bright red beak, which it uses to snatch fish.

Did you find them all?

Zebra mussel
This striped little mollusk is native to the Caspian Sea, meaning that this is its original home. In other countries around the world, the zebra mussel is an unpopular fast-breeding pest that destroys local, native species.

Whooper swans

Little is known about these snowy birds that visit the Caspian Sea. They are believed to breed in the cold, barren lands of Siberia before flying south for warmer weather.

The people helping

Blue Marine Foundation and a local NGO called IDEA are working together with the government and local communities in Azerbaijan to protect the Caspian Sea's critically endangered sturgeon. Together, they are supporting the first marine park here, which will stop illegal fishing and limit pollution of the waters.

Great reserves of oil and gas lie beneath the Caspian Sea, so many of its shores are lined with big oil businesses. Oil spills threaten the health and survival of seals, birds, and other wildlife that get stuck in this deadly water pollution.

Giant Caspian salmon

This critically endangered fish is a piscivore, which means that its main diet is fish.

Greater flamingo

Flamingos are actually born with white-gray feathers. Their pink color comes from the food they eat, so it takes years for them to turn pink.

Caspian turtle

The Caspian turtle's yellowy shell has black patches that help it blend in with its sandy home on the shore, where it dips in and out of shallow waters to catch a meal.

How you can help

Clean, renewable energy like solar, wind, and waves is much better for the environment. Find out if your home or school can switch to these greener energy sources and help keep oil and gas in the ground.

Caspian lamprey

This eel-like fish is anadromous, which means it lives in both saltwater and freshwater. It is rare, because river dams block its path and prevent it from mating, and droughts are drying the streams it lives in.

Sea walnut

Sea walnuts are slow-moving, and they cannot see. They can't chase their prey, so they have to be sneaky. They use tiny hairs called cilia to create currents that pull their prey into their mouths.

Can you find them all?

- Sea angel
- Basket star
- Arctic comb jelly

Alaska

Under the Alaskan summer sun, humpback whales are gathered close to the ocean's surface, blowing air and surfing forward as a pod. They have a plan. Above them, seabirds are circling noisily, watching the chase. The whales slow and, together, they dive. Their tails upend as they plunge straight down into the water. Below the surface, a school of panicked herring find themselves surrounded. The whales are blowing bubbles, forcing the herring into an ever-tighter ball. Then, in a perfectly coordinated move, the humpback whales surge upward. They fill their huge, wide mouths with fish, and as they break the water's surface, the seabirds dive in to join the feast too.

The habitat

There is no land at the North Pole; only sea ice. This freezes and melts as the seasons change. Between October and June, most of the Arctic Ocean is covered by ice.

Sea ice
Parts of the Arctic Ocean's surface remain frozen all year

Because of the Earth's tilt, the sun does not set at the North Pole in summer. So in Arctic summers, phytoplankton bloom. These tiny ocean organisms are the foundation of an amazing web of Arctic life, including fish, seals, birds, whales, and polar bears.

Beluga whale
These pure white whales hunt fish. Although they have teeth, beluga whales prefer to gulp their prey whole.

Herring
Each female herring can lay up to 60,000 eggs. When they are spawning, the ocean floor is covered in a dense carpet of eggs that take only a week to hatch.

Arctic Ocean

The Arctic Ocean is the world's shallowest and smallest ocean. It is the most northern ocean on Earth. "Arctic" comes from the Greek word "Arktos," which means "bear." The name is thought to refer to the Little Bear and Great Bear star constellations that can be seen in the sky here.

Shorthorn sculpin
Male shorthorn sculpins are attentive parents. Once the female has laid her eggs, the males stay nearby to protect them for up to three months.

Ribbon seal
Ribbon seal pups are born with thick, woolly white coats. They get their adult black and white banding when they are about three years old.

Did you find them all?

Sea angel
This swimming sea slug flaps its underwater wings to find its prey. It is looking for a sea snail called a sea butterfly. The sea angel grasps the sea butterfly and sucks it out whole from its shell.

Walrus

Walruses have two special air sacs in their throat that store air and make it possible for them to float vertically in the water and even take a nap.

As whales swim and dive, they help mix up the nutrients on the surface of the ocean with those in the deep. This makes food available to different marine animals at different depths. Whale poop is also important too. It feeds phytoplankton, which then take carbon dioxide out of the air and produce the oxygen we breathe. So by helping phytoplankton grow, whales are also helping fight climate change!

Narwhal

Narwhals are often called "unicorns of the sea." They have a long tusk sticking forward from their heads. The tusk is actually a tooth that can grow up to 9 ft 11 in (3 m) long!

Skeleton shrimp

Sometimes called the "praying mantis of the seas," skeleton shrimp have five pairs of legs: two pairs at their front end and three more pairs at their back end.

Polar bear

Polar bears have two layers of fur and a thick layer of fat. They even have tufts of fur between their toes!

The people helping

Whale and Dolphin Conservation (WDC) are determined to end the captivity of all whales and dolphins who are imprisoned for entertainment. These gentle, social marine animals are stressed by being confined in tanks and made to perform, so WDC are campaigning for their release.

How you can help

Venues that keep whales and dolphins captive for live shows depend on paying visitors. By refusing to visit places that keep marine mammals for entertainment, you can help end the captivity of these wild ocean creatures.

Basket star

In the darkness of the ocean floor, this delicate creature unfolds. It waves its arms in the current, trying to catch a meal. Should a beam of light find it, the basket star folds back into a little knotted ball.

Arctic comb jelly

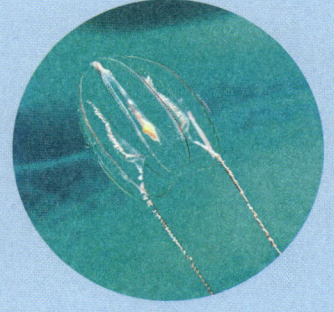

Unlike most jellyfish, the Arctic comb jelly prefers cold water. Light reflects off its transparent body, so it shimmers with the colors of the rainbow.

Yellowstone River

Yellowstone Park is shrouded in a white haze as winter closes in. Trees droop with snow, and mist rises from the Yellowstone River as it starts to freeze. On the riverbank, a family of otters tumble and play, oblivious to the plunging temperatures. They know their thick, dark coats will protect them in the coming months. Icicles hang off the shaggy coats of the bison patrolling the surrounding grassland, their breath steaming in the cold air. Above them, on a branch arching over the water, a bald eagle surveys the scene. Her bright eyes flash as she scans the river's dark, icy water for trout and other fish to snatch for a tasty dinner.

Can you find them all?

 Western tiger salamander

 Gray catbird

 Cutthroat trout

Habitat

The Yellowstone River winds for hundreds of miles across the US states of Wyoming, Montana, and North Dakota. It flows through Yellowstone National Park in flat-bottomed valleys carved out of this dramatic landscape.

Winter brings plunging temperatures to Yellowstone Park, and the Yellowstone River often freezes. Come spring, mountain meltwater floods the river. In summer, the park's elk, bison, and wolves are able to make easier and safer crossings between the river's wide banks.

Downhill flow
Rivers can only flow downhill because of gravity.

Elk
The Native American word for elk is "wapiti," which means light-colored deer. Elk are related to deer but are much larger.

Beaver
By making dams on the river, beavers change and slow the flow of the water. This creates new freshwater habitats that attract different wildlife, from plants to fish and frogs.

Undammed river

Yellowstone River is the longest undammed river in the United States. River dams are built by humans to control how river waters flow. They can be useful for producing electricity or for preventing flooding in surrounding areas. However, they also disrupt wildlife and habitats. That's why people have campaigned for the Yellowstone River to stay undammed.

Grizzly bear
Grizzly bears hibernate for up to seven months of the year. During this time, they don't even go to the bathroom!

Mountain bluebird
This little bird's name inspired the phrase "bluebird days," which refers to cloudless, sunny weather with bright blue skies.

Did you find them all?

Western tiger salamander
This salamander lays its eggs in Yellowstone Lake. After maturing for between two and five months, the young salamander crawls out to live on land and start the cycle again.

American white pelican
These birds have a huge wingspan of almost 6 ft 7 in (2 m) across. Their large, webbed feet and strong legs help them paddle in the river.

The people helping
National Park rangers track wildlife throughout the park and collect evidence of what is happening. They then use science to make plans to protect the park and the animals and plants that live there.

Wolves in Yellowstone Park were hunted until there were none left. But then the numbers of elk—the wolves' main prey—boomed. The elk grazed until the valleys and riverbanks were bare. Then, in 1995, wolves were reintroduced with dramatic effect. They preyed on the elk, whose numbers fell. With elk now always on the move, more trees grew, which stabilized the riverbanks. In time, the path of the river changed as beavers, songbirds, and bears returned.

Bison
Once close to extinction, thousands of bison now roam Yellowstone Park. This is the only place in the world where bison have wandered the grasslands since prehistoric times.

Gray wolf
The prey of the gray wolf includes large mammals, such as elk and bison, as well as beavers and rodents. Adult wolves can eat up to 20 lb (9 kg) of meat in a single meal!

How you can help
If you've been inspired by the positive impact of rewilding in Yellowstone Park, why not find out how you can create wilder and more diverse habitats in your garden to encourage more local wildlife? If you don't have a garden at home, look out for rewilding projects in local parks.

Gray catbird
This little songbird gets its name from the catlike "meow" noise it makes. It also mimics the songs of other birds and can even make two different sounds at the same time!

Cutthroat trout
These native fish are food for more than 16 species of birds and mammals. In April, they migrate upstream to spawn. The clean, oxygen-rich waters here are what the eggs need to hatch.

Glossary

Have you seen any new words during your adventures? Use this glossary to learn their meaning.

adapted
When a living thing is able to survive somewhere because it has changed over time

algae
An organism usually found in water that can perform photosynthesis

altitude
The height above sea level. Low altitude means closer to sea level; high altitude means farther away from sea level

amphibian
Small vertebrates that can only survive in water or in a moist environment

aquatic
Living, growing, or happening in water

by-catch
Sea creatures that are caught accidentally when fishing

canopy
The second highest level of a forest. It is thick with leaves and branches and protects the lower levels of the forest from rain, sun, and wind

carnivore
An animal that eats other animals or a plant that eats small animals, such as insects

conservation
Protecting the world's natural resources so they continue to exist

crustacean
Animals that have a hard outer shell and live in water

ecosystem
How all the organisms and the environment in a geographical area work together. Ecosystems have living parts—such as plants and animals—and nonliving parts, such as rocks and the climate

endangered
A species that is at risk of extinction

endemic
A plant or animal that can only be found in one place

evaporation
The process when liquid turns into gas

extinct
A species that no longer exists, such as dinosaurs

floodwater
Water that has been left behind by flooding

freshwater
Any water that occurs naturally and doesn't have a lot of salt in it, such as rivers and lakes

groundwater
Water that is held in rocks and soil underground

habitat
The place that animals, plants, and other organisms call home

hibernate
To spend the winter sleeping

invasive
A plant or animal that arrives in a new place and is harmful to its new setting

meltwater
Water made up of melted ice or snow

migrate
Moving from one place to another, usually when seasons change

mollusk
An animal with no spine, a soft body, and usually covered in a shell

native
A person, animal, or plant that originally comes from a place and occurs there naturally

NGO
An organization that is not controlled by the goverment. NGOs usually have political or social aims

nocturnal
Something that happens or is active at nighttime

nutrients
Any substances that plants and animals need to survive and grow

organisms
A single living thing, such as a plant or animal

plankton
Organisms that are carried along by the tide or currents in water

poaching
Illegally hunting or catching wild animals on land where this isn't allowed

predator
An animal that naturally preys on other animals

prehistoric
The time before written records

saltwater
Water that has salt in it

sand mining
The activity of removing sand from the shores of lakes and rivers or from seabeds

sea anemone
A brightly coloured sea creature that lives on underwater rocks

spawn
Lay eggs

species
A type of animal or plant

stalactite
A rock that hangs down from the roof of a cave

sustainably
A way of doing things that does as little harm to the environment as possible and so can continue for a long time

toxin
A substance that is poisonous

trawling
Pulling a large net through deep sea to catch fish

venomous
An animal that can inject venom when it bites or stings

vertebrate
Any animal that has a backbone inside its body

Animal index

 Arctic comb jelly
81, 83

 Black rhino
23

 Arctic tern
58

 Blue-footed booby
49, 51

 African bullfrog
20, 23

 Ascension frigatebird
41, 43

 Blue marlin
41, 42

 African elephant
20, 22

 Ascension spurge
42

 Blue tang
40-41, 42

 African penguin
52, 54

 Bank cormorant
52, 55

 Blue whale
65, 66

 African wild dog
21, 22

 Basket star
81, 83

 Brine shrimp
52, 55

 Albacore tuna
10

 Beaver
84, 86

 Bromeliads
36-37, 39

 Albatross
57, 59

 Beluga sturgeon
78

 Brotula eel
60-61, 63

 Albino crustacean
60, 63

 Beluga whale
82

 Brown pelican
66

 Amazon whipsnake
39

 Bigeye tuna
18

 California sea lion
67

 American white pelican
87

 Bioluminescent lanternfish
16-17, 18

 Cape gannets
53, 54

 Anchovies
64, 66

 Bison
84, 87

 Caspian gull
76-77, 78

 Andean geese
46

 Black-lip pearl oyster
11

 Caspian lamprey
76, 79

 Antarctic silverfish
34

 Black mangrove
74

 Caspian tern
77, 78

 Antarctic toothfish
58

 Black-necked stork
28, 31

 Caspian turtle
77, 79

 Catfish
45, 46

 Catshark
25, 27

 Cave Molly
60-61, 62

 Climbing salamander
37, 38

 Coconut crab
11

 Colossal squid
32, 34

 Common cuttlefish
25, 26

 Common lobster
27

 Conger eel
25, 26

 Coral
10

 Crocodile icefish
56, 59

 Crown-of-thorns starfish
75

 Cutthroat trout
84-85, 87

 Cuttlefish eggs
24-25, 27

 Damara tern
55

 Damselfly
37, 39

 Devil ray
65, 66

 Diving beetle
36-37, 39

 Dolphin
27

 Dusky dolphin
55

 Eastern blue devil fish
69, 71

 Elk
85, 86

 Emperor penguin
56, 59

 European bass
26

 False killer whale
71

 Flatback sea turtle
70

 Flying fish
40-41, 43

 Galápagos lava lizard
49, 51

 Galápagos penguin
48-49, 51

 Gangetic dolphin
28, 31

 Gharial
28, 30

 Giant anaconda
14

 Giant Antarctic sea spider
56-57, 58

 Giant Caspian salmon
76-77, 79

 Giant grouper
73, 74

 Glass frog
39

 Glass sponge
33, 35

 Glittering-throated emerald hummingbird
39

 Greater flamingo
79

 Great frigatebird
9, 11

 Great white shark
16, 18

 Green sea turtle
40, 43

 Gray catbird
84-85, 87

 Gray reef shark
72, 74

 Gray seal
24, 26

 Gray wolf
87

 Grizzly bear
86

 Guitarfish
72-73, 75

 Hammerhead shark
64, 66

 Harpy eagle
13, 15

 Hawksbill sea turtle
9, 10

 Hells Bells stalactite
60-61, 62

 Heaviside's dolphin
53, 54

 Heleobia
44-45, 47

 Herring
80, 82

 Hippopotamus
21, 22

 Hoff crab
59

 Honeycomb moray eel
11, 72, 74

 Humboldt squid
64, 67

 Humpback red snapper
75

 Indian leopard
29, 30

 Indian wolf
29, 30

 Indian skimmer
28, 31

 Indo-Pacific bottlenose dolphin
70

 Jaguar
12-13, 14

 Jumping spider
36, 38

 Karachi fish
44-45, 46

 Krill
35, 57

 Lake Titicaca giant frog
44-45, 46

 Large painted locust
48, 50

 Lava heron
48-49, 51

 Lesser flamingo
52, 54

 Leatherback sea turtle
64, 67

 Leopard seal
56, 58

 Lily-trotter
21, 23

 Lion
22

 Lionfish
9, 10

 Loggerhead sea turtle
18-19

 Macaroni penguin
57, 59

 Mako shark
16, 18

 Many-colored rush tyrant
47

 Marine iguana
48-49, 50

 Marsh crocodile
29, 31

 May flower
14-15

 Medusa jellyfish
17, 19

 Mexican free-tailed bat
60-61, 62

 Mexican mealybug
63

 Mexican tetra fish
60-61, 63

 Minke whale
34

 Mosquito larvae
36-37, 38

 Mountain bluebird
86

 Narwhal
83

 Nile monitor
21, 23

 Oaxaca cave sleeper
61, 63

 Ocean sunfish
17, 19, 51

 Orca
53, 64, 66

 Orinoco crocodile
14

 Parrotfish
8-9, 11

 Pel's fishing owl
21, 23

 Phytoplankton
16, 19

 Polar bear
83

 Polka-dot tree frog
36, 38

 Prickly pear cactus
49, 51

 Procaris ascensionis
40, 43

 Rainbow trout
44, 47

 Rare short-snouted seahorse
24-25, 27

 Red-crowned roofed turtle
28-29, 31

 Reddish hermit hummingbird
12, 15

 Red howler monkey
12, 15

 Red lechwe
20, 23

 Red-lipped batfish
50

 Reef manta ray
75

 Resplendent pygmy angelfish
41, 43

 Ribbon seal
82

 Roraima rocket frog
12-13, 15

 Ruddy shelduck
29, 30

 Sally Lightfoot crab
48-49, 50

 Sardines
52, 54

 Sarus crane
28, 30

 Sea angel
80-81, 82

 Sea butterfly
32-33, 35

 Seagrass
72-73, 74

 Sea squirt
35

 Sea star
33, 35

 Sea walnut
76-77, 79

 Shorthorn sculpin
81, 82

 Sixgill shark
40, 42

 Skeleton shrimp
83

 Smooth-coated otter
28-29, 31

 Snake sea cucumber
72-73, 75

 Snow petrel
57, 58

 Sooty tern
40-41, 42

 Southern fur seal
52, 54

 Southern right whale
55

 Southern stoplight loosejaw
68-69, 70

 Sperm whale
19

 Spider crab
24, 26

 Squat lobster
33, 35

 Staghorn coral
8-9, 10-11

 Strawberry poison frog
36, 38

 Strawberry squid
19

 Sugar kelp
24-25, 27

 Sundew plant
14

 Swallows
62

 Termites
20-21, 22

 Titicaca grebe
45, 47

 Totoaba
64-65, 67

 Totora
46

 Triton conch
75

 Vaquita
65, 67

 Vicuña
47

 Yellow-banded poison dart frog
15

 Yellowfin tuna
41, 43

 Yellow-red rat snake
63

 Yellow sea lily
32-33, 35

 Walrus
83

 Weddell seal
34

 Weedy seadragon
68-69, 71

 Western tiger salamander
84-85, 86

 Whale barnacles
57, 59

 Whale shark
8-9, 10

 White-faced storm petrel
71

 White lady fish
60, 62

 White sea anemone
32, 34

 Whitetip reef shark
50

 Whooper swan
77, 79

 Wild guinea pig
47

 Zebra mussel
76-77, 78

Acknowledgements

DK would like to thank Jude Brown, Vivienne Evans, Sam Fanshawe, Shaha Hashim, Anna Hughes, Rory Moore, and the rest of the team at Blue Marine Foundation.

Picture Credits

The publisher would like to thank the following for their kind permission to reproduce their photographs:
(Key: a-above; b-below/bottom; c-centre; f-far; l-left; r-right; t-top)

10 Dreamstime.com: Andrey Armyagov (cra); Krzysztof Odziomek / Crisod (cb); Dirk Jan Mattaar (bc). Getty Images: tororo (tc). 11 Alamy Stock Photo: Patrick J. Endres (bc). Dreamstime.com: Gary Webber (cl); Steven Melanson / Xscream1 (cb). naturepl.com: Roland Seitre (bl). 14 Alamy Stock Photo: Gerard Lacz / mauritius images GmbH (cr). Dreamstime.com: Cosmopol (tc); Hin255 (bc). Getty Images: Julian Gunther (cb). 15 Alamy Stock Photo: Ch'ien Lee / Minden Pictures (bc). Dreamstime.com: Rafael Cerqueira (bl); Jesse Kraft / Jkraft5 (cb). naturepl.com: Luke Massey (tl). 18 Alamy Stock Photo: Nature Picture Library (cb); Tim Hall / Cultura RM (cr). Getty Images / iStock: vladoskan (cr). naturepl.com: Solvin Zankl (bc). 19 123RF.com: Micha Klootwijk / michaklootwijk (bc). Alamy Stock Photo: Doug Perrine (clb). Dreamstime.com: Bidouze Stphane / Smithore (bl). Getty Images / iStock: tonaquatic (tl). 22 Alamy Stock Photo: AfriPics.com (bc); Angelo Cavalli / robertharding (tc). Dreamstime.com: Ecophoto (crb); Sergey Uryadnikov (ca). 23 Alamy Stock Photo: blickwinkel / McPHOTO / M. Schaef (bl); Wim van den Heever / Nature Picture Library (cb). Dreamstime.com: Patrice Correia (bc). Getty Images: Paul Morigi / Getty Images for National Geographic (tc). naturepl.com: Neil Aldridge (cla). 26 Alamy Stock Photo: Alex Mustard / 2020VISION / Nature Picture Library (c). Dorling Kindersley: David Peart (bc). Dreamstime.com: Goran afarek (cra). naturepl.com: Alex Mustard (tc). 27 Alamy Stock Photo: Alex Mustard / Nature Picture Library (cla); Emily Bulled, Blue Marine Foundation (tfr); Sue Daly / Nature Picture Library (bl). naturepl.com: Linda Pitkin / 2020VISION (cb); Lewis Jefferies (bc). 30 Dreamstime.com: Richard Lindie (ca); Elena Odareeva (tc); Yezhenliang (bc). naturepl.com: Francois Savigny (crb). 31 Alamy Stock Photo: Rakesh Dhareshwar (bl); Arco / C. Htter / Imagebroker (cla). Dreamstime.com: Klodien (tc). naturepl.com: Axel Gomille (cb); Roland Seitre (bc). 34 Dorling Kindersley: Linda Pitkin (bc). Dreamstime.com: Vladimir Melnik / Zanskar (cra). Getty Images: Michael Nolan / robertharding (tc). naturepl.com: Juergen Freund (cb). 35 Alamy Stock Photo: GRANGER - Historical Picture Archive (tc). Dorling Kindersley: David Peart (cla). Dreamstime.com: Feathercollector (bl); Kelpfish (cb); Sergey Frolov (bc). 38 123RF.com: James Anak Anthony Collin / telomato (cra). Alamy Stock Photo: Nature Picture Library (bc); Morley Read (tc). Dreamstime.com: Dirk Ercken (cb). 39 Alamy Stock Photo: Glenn Bartley / All Canada Photos (cl). Dreamstime.com: Marekkijevsky (bl); Mgkuijpers (cb); Viter8 (cr). 42 Alamy Stock Photo: WaterFrame (cb). Dreamstime.com: Stevebb (cra). Shutterstock.com: Gaid Kornsilapa (cb); Alexander Trybushny (tc). 43 Alamy Stock Photo: Alf Jacob Nilsen (clb); Will Wood (tfr); Jeff Rotman (bc). Dreamstime.com: Shane Myers (cla). Getty Images: Brent Barnes / Stocktrek Images (bl). 46 Alamy Stock Photo: Christian GUY / imageBROKER (cb); Bert Willaert / Nature Picture Library (cra). Dreamstime.com: Lucia Collazos Gonzalez (bl); Paologozzi (tc). 47 Alamy Stock Photo: blickwinkel / AGAMI / D. Shapiro (bl); Arco / G. Lacz / Imagebroker (t!); Charles Mann (tc); PAUL R. STERRY / Nature Photographers Ltd (bc). naturepl.com: Alex Mustard / 2020VISION (cb). 50 Dorling Kindersley: Linda Pitkin (cb). Dreamstime.com: Uwe Bergwitz (bc); Jesse Kraft (tc); Michael Zysman (cra). 51 Alamy Stock Photo: Gary and Donna Brewer (bc); Michael Nolan / robertharding (bl). Dreamstime.com: Oreena (cb). Fotolia: Impala (cla). 54 Dreamstime.com: Aquanaut4 (bc); Nicola Messana (tc). Getty Images / iStock: spooh (ca). 55 Alamy Stock Photo: mike lane (bc); Chris & Monique Fallows / Nature Picture Library (clb). 58 Alamy Stock Photo: Norbert Wu / Minden Pictures (bc). Dreamstime.com: Agami Photo Agency (cb); Alexey Sedov (cr). naturepl.com: Stefan Christmann (tc). 59 Dreamstime.com: Richard Lindie (bc). Getty Images / iStock: KeithSzafranski (cla). naturepl.com: Jordi Chias (cb); Doc White (bl). 62 Alamy Stock Photo: Michael Durham / Nature Picture Library (cr); Claudio Contreras / Nature Picture Library (bc). Dreamstime.com: C © sar Ezequiel Garrido (tc); Verastuchelova (cb). 63 Alamy Stock Photo: Robbie Shone / Design Pics - Brand B (cla); LITTLE DINOSAUR (bc). Dreamstime.com: Matthijs Kuijpers (c). naturepl.com: Albert Lleal (bl). 66 Alamy Stock Photo: Doc White / Nature Picture Library (cra); Norbert Wu / Minden Pictures (bc). Dreamstime.com: Ruth Peterkin (tc); Sergey Uryadnikov (cb). 67 Alamy Stock Photo: Nature Picture Library (bl); Richard Herrmann / Minden Pictures (bc). Dreamstime.com: Stephanie Rousseau / Stephanierousseau (clb). Getty Images / iStock: Michael Zeigler (cl). Shutterstock.com: oksana.perkins (tc). 70 Alamy Stock Photo: Jonathon David Imagery (tc); Doug Perrine (cb). Dreamstime.com: Shawn Jackson / Shawnjackson (cr). naturepl.com: Solvin Zankl (bc). 71 Alamy Stock Photo: blickwinkel / AGAMI / D. Occhiato (cla); Mark Conlin (bl). naturepl.com: Gary Bell / Oceanwide (bc). 74 Dreamstime.com: Czuber (tc); Prillfoto (cra). Getty Images: Reinhard Dirscherl / ullstein bild (cb). naturepl.com: Alex Mustard (bc). 75 Alamy Stock Photo: cbimages (bl); Viv Evans, Blue Marine Foundation (tfr); Reinhard Dirscherl (cl); WaterFrame_dpr (cb); Norbert Probst / imageBROKER (bc). 78 Alamy Stock Photo: Juan Vilata (tc). Dreamstime.com: Dirkr (cb); Rostislav Stefanek (cr). Getty Images: Ed Reschke (cb). 79 Rory Moore, Blue Marine Foundation (tfr); Alamy Stock Photo: Alex Mustard / naturepl.com (bc). Dreamstime.com: Menno67 (cla); Paolo Del Ponte (cb). Shutterstock.com: Manuel E. Garci (bl). 82 Alamy Stock Photo: Zoonar / Dmytro Pylypenko (tc). Dreamstime.com: Mandimiles (cr). naturepl.com: Aflo (cb); Franco Banfi (bc). 83 Alamy Stock Photo: Franco Banfi / Biosphoto (bc); Theo Allofs / Minden Pictures (cla); Georgette Apol / Steve Bloom Images (bl). Dreamstime.com: Alexey Sedov (cb). 86 Alamy Stock Photo: Andrew DuBois (bc). Dreamstime.com: Bruce Beck (tc). Getty Images / iStock: BirdofPrey (cb); Matt Dirksen (cr). 87 Alamy Stock Photo: Graycat bird (bl). Dreamstime.com: Geoffrey Kuchera (cb); Silviu Matei / Silviumatei (cla). naturepl.com: Charlie Summers (bc). Shutterstock.com: Peter Bowman (tc) Cover images: Back: Dreamstime.com: Uwe Bergwitz (crb), Shane Myers (clb), Shawn Jackson / Shawnjackson tc, Sergey Uryadnikov (tl); naturepl.com: Alex Mustard / 2020VISION (cra). 95 Blue Marine Foundation. All other images © Dorling Kindersley.

Editor Vicky Armstrong
Americanization Editor Kayla Dugger
Project Art Editor Jon Hall
Designer Christine Keilty
Senior Picture Researcher Sakshi Saluja
Production Editor Marc Staples
Senior Production Controller Louise Minihane
Senior Acquisitions Editor Katy Flint
Managing Art Editor Vicky Short
Publishing Director Mark Searle

Written by Catherine Barr
Illustrated by Riley Samels

First American Edition, 2023
Published in the United States by DK Publishing, in association with Blue Marine Foundation.
DK, 1745 Broadway, 20th Floor, New York, NY 10019

Page design copyright © 2023 Dorling Kindersley Limited
Text copyright © Catherine Barr, 2023
Illustrations copyright © Riley Samels, 2023

DK, a Division of Penguin Random House LLC
23 24 25 26 27 10 9 8 7 6 5 4 3 2 1
001–334948–August/2023

All rights reserved. Without limiting the rights under the copyright reserved above, no part of this publication may be reproduced, stored in or introduced into a retrieval system, or transmitted, in any form, or by any means (electronic, mechanical, photocopying, recording, or otherwise), without the prior written permission of the copyright owner.
Published in Great Britain by Dorling Kindersley Limited.

A catalog record for this book is available from the Library of Congress.
ISBN 978-0-7440-8173-2

DK books are available at special discounts when purchased in bulk for sales promotions, premiums, fundraising, or educational use. For details, contact: DK Publishing Special Markets, 1745 Broadway, 20th Floor, New York, NY 10019
SpecialSales@dk.com

Printed and bound in Slovakia

For the curious
www.dk.com

This book was made with Forest Stewardship Council™ certified paper—one small step in DK's commitment to a sustainable future. For more information go to www.dk.com/our-green-pledge